GARDENING
DIFFICULTIES SOLVED

EXPERT ANSWERS TO
AMATEUR'S QUESTIONS

Edited By

H. H. THOMAS

First published in 1910

British Library Cataloguing-in-Publication Data
A catalogue record for this book is available
from the British Library

A Short History of Gardening

Gardening is the practice of growing and cultivating plants as part of horticulture more broadly. In most domestic gardens, there are two main sets of plants; 'ornamental plants', grown for their flowers, foliage or overall appearance – and 'useful plants' such as root vegetables, leaf vegetables, fruits and herbs, grown for consumption or other uses. For many people, gardening is an incredibly relaxing and rewarding pastime, ranging from caring for large fruit orchards to residential yards including lawns, foundation plantings or flora in simple containers. Gardening is separated from farming or forestry more broadly in that it tends to be much more labour-intensive; involving active participation in the growing of plants.

Home-gardening has an incredibly long history, rooted in the 'forest gardening' practices of prehistoric times. In the gradual process of families improving their immediate environment, useful tree and vine species were identified, protected and improved whilst undesirable species were eliminated. Eventually foreign species were also selected and incorporated into the 'gardens.' It was only after the emergence of the first civilisations that wealthy individuals began to create gardens for aesthetic purposes. Egyptian tomb paintings from around 1500 BC provide some of the earliest physical evidence of ornamental horticulture and landscape design; depicting lotus ponds surrounded by symmetrical rows of acacias and palms. A notable example of an ancient ornamental garden was the 'Hanging Gardens of Babylon' – one of the Seven Wonders of the Ancient World.

Ancient Rome had dozens of great gardens, and Roman estates tended to be laid out with hedges and vines and contained a wide variety of flowers – acanthus, cornflowers, crocus, cyclamen, hyacinth, iris, ivy, lavender, lilies, myrtle, narcissus, poppy, rosemary and violets as well as statues and sculptures. Flower beds were also popular in the courtyards of rich Romans. The Middle Ages represented a period of decline for gardens with aesthetic purposes however. After the fall of Rome gardening was done with the purpose of growing medicinal herbs and/or decorating church altars. It was mostly monasteries that carried on the tradition of garden design and horticultural techniques during the medieval period in Europe. By the late thirteenth century, rich Europeans began to grow gardens for leisure as well as for medicinal herbs and vegetables. They generally surrounded them with walls – hence, the 'walled garden.'

These gardens advanced by the sixteenth and seventeenth centuries into symmetrical, proportioned and balanced designs with a more classical appearance. Gardens in the renaissance were adorned with sculptures (in a nod to Roman heritage), topiary and fountains. These fountains often contained 'water jokes' – hidden cascades which suddenly soaked visitors. The most famous fountains of this kind were found in the Villa d'Este (1550-1572) at Tivoli near Rome. By the late seventeenth century, European gardeners had started planting new flowers such as tulips, marigolds and sunflowers.

These highly complex designs, largely created by the aristocracy slowly gave way to the individual gardener however – and this is where this book comes in! Cottage Gardens first emerged during the Elizabethan times, originally created by poorer workers to provide themselves with food and herbs, with flowers planted amongst them for decoration. Farm workers were generally provided with cottages set in a small garden— about an acre—where they could grow food, keep pigs, chickens and often bees; the latter necessitating the planting of decorative pollen flora. By Elizabethan times there was more prosperity, and thus more room to grow flowers. Most of the early cottage garden flowers would have had practical uses though —violets were spread on the floor (for their pleasant scent and keeping out vermin); calendulas and primroses were both attractive and used in cooking. Others, such as sweet william and hollyhocks were grown entirely for their beauty.

Here lies the roots of today's home-gardener; further influenced by the 'new style' in eighteenth century England which replaced the more formal, symmetrical 'Garden à la française'. Such gardens, close to works of art, were often inspired by paintings in the classical style of landscapes by Claude Lorraine and Nicolas Poussin. The work of Lancelot 'Capability' Brown, described as 'England's greatest gardener' was particularly influential. We hope that the reader is inspired by this book, and the long and varied history of gardening itself, to experiment with some home-gardening of their own. Enjoy.

PREFACE

It is commonly acknowledged that the Questions and Answers columns of a gardening paper contain information that is invaluable to its readers generally. The questions are asked by amateurs and answered by experts. The replies are useful not only to the actual inquirers but to all amateurs, for the trials and troubles of one inexperienced gardener are very similar to those of another. Thus the suggestion that a careful selection of Questions and Answers from the columns of THE GARDENER would be welcomed in book form was not made without good grounds. This suggestion prompted the preparation of "Gardening Difficulties Solved."

The information given in the following pages is practical and to the point, and, it is hoped, will meet all ordinary difficulties that confront the possessor of a garden. The questions have actually been asked by amateurs, so that the troubles they voice are real. Since conditions of climate influence gardening work to a considerable degree, the district from which each question was sent is indicated.

H. H. T.

January, 1910.

CONTENTS

THE MOUNTAIN CLEMATIS (CLEMATIS MONTANA) ON A COTTAGE IN YORKSHIRE. TO PRUNE, CUT OUT SOME OF THE OLD SHOOTS AS SOON AS THE FLOWERS ARE OVER.

GARDENING DIFFICULTIES SOLVED

CHAPTER I

The Beginner's Guide to Rose Growing

Time to Plant Roses

Q. When should Roses be planted? I have been advised that various times are the best, and should be glad to know definitely.— *E. S., Bucks.*

A. The best time is during the last week in October and the first two weeks in November. If, however, the ground is very wet the Roses should not be planted but laid in a shallow trench, the roots being well covered with soil. This is commonly spoken of as "laying in" or "heeling in." In such circumstances the Roses are planted when the soil is dry enough to be dug without sticking together in big lumps. Roses may be planted from the end of October until the end of March, or in northern counties until the middle of April. It is better to plant later in ground that is in suitable condition than to plant early in ground that is saturated. If Roses in pots are bought they may be planted at any time up to June, for there is no need to disturb the roots to any appreciable extent. They are, however, more expensive than Roses lifted from the open ground.

How to Plant

Q. How shall I proceed to plant Roses? Is it necessary to use manure at planting time?—*J. K. L., Romford.*

A. The chief thing to do is to dig the ground at least 2 feet deep. Roses are not successful in badly tilled ground. Well rotted farmyard manure is the best stuff to dig in the Rose beds before planting, and it should be mixed in the lower 12 inches, so as not to be in direct contact with the roots at first. If this cannot be had, basic slag, applied at the rate of 8 oz. per square yard, may be used. It is best to prepare the ground two or three weeks before the Roses are

B

put in, so that it may settle down to its normal level. Put in the Roses so that the junction of stock and scion is covered with 1 inch of soil.

It is most important (*a*) to cut off all bruised and broken ends, (*b*) to spread out the roots to their full extent, (*c*) to work the soil well amongst them, and (*d*) to make the soil quite firm by treading. Do not put all the soil in and then make firm, but tread down each spadeful as it is put in. The uppermost roots of standard and climbing Roses should be about 2 inches below the surface ; the stake is put in before the soil. It is of great importance to make standards firm and to secure them to a stake or other support. Otherwise they get blown about and loosened.

Replanting Roses

Q. I am desirous of replanting some Rose trees in a fresh position this year. The trees have borne a very good supply of blooms and appear to be strong. When would be the best time to undertake this ? and should the trees be pruned before or after they have been transplanted ?—*Unimus, Surrey.*

A. The best time to undertake the work of replanting your Roses would be in the latter part of October or early November. As you dig up the trees, cut back the roots a few inches with a sharp knife, and look well for suckers of the wild stock on which they are budded. If any are seen, cut them off at the point of origin. The growths should be cut back to about 15 or 18 inches from the base. Dip the roots at once in some thin mud, and cover them with soil in a shady place until you are prepared to replant. Choose fine weather for the replanting. The plants will take no harm heeled in for a week or two provided the soil is well trodden about their roots.

Planting Sweet Briar for Hedge

Q. Will you advise me as to the distance apart at which I should plant Sweet Briar Roses to form a hedge ? Also whether the Penzance Briars are as sweet smelling as the Common Sweet Briar ?— *A. O. C., Altrincham.*

A. If you are planting a single row, a distance of about 2 feet should be allowed between the plants of common Sweet Briars, and $2\frac{1}{2}$ feet for Penzance Briars. If a wide hedge is desired then plant a double row thus . · . · , the plants 18 inches apart. The Penzance Briars are very sweet in foliage, but not quite equal to the common Sweet Briar. They are, however, most lovely when in bloom.

A GATHERING OF RED AND YELLOW ROSES.

Pruning Hybrid Perpetual Roses

Q. I have a collection of Hybrid Perpetual Roses, but the pruning has been neglected.   Can you advise ?—*E. J., Hitchin.*

A. These are easily divided into three sections representative of their vigour of growth, namely weak (*e.g.* A. K. Williams) ; moderate (*e.g.* Mrs. John Laing) ; vigorous (*e.g.* Clio).   They should be pruned according to their growth — the stronger the shoots are, the less severe pruning they need. Pruning encourages growth, so that to cut back a vigorous shoot hard results in the production of three or four equally strong growths with fewer flowers. Broadly speaking, the vigorous sorts are cut back to within 9 inches or 1 foot

BUSH OF HYBRID TEA ROSE BEFORE
PRUNING.

of the base of the previous year's growth.   Those of moderate growth may be cut back to within 6 inches, and the weak growers to within 2 to 4 inches of the base of the previous summer's growth.

Pruning Hybrid Tea Roses

Q. How far back should I cut my Hybrid Tea Roses at pruning ? —*X. Y. Z., Henley.*

A. These are essentially the Roses for the garden, especially for the town and suburban garden. They should only be moderately pruned. The strong growths may be left 1 foot to 18 inches in length, or even more if large bushes are desirable. Shorten the side or lateral growths to within 2 to 3 inches of the main shoots. The weak growing Hybrid Teas require more severe pruning; Liberty and Mildred Grant are examples.

Pruning Tea and China Roses

Q. I am in doubt as to the proper method of pruning Tea and China Roses. Please advise.— *H. W., Sussex.*

A. These Roses often suffer rather severely from frost except where well protected or in sheltered positions. After the injured shoots

THE SAME PLANT AS IT APPEARS AFTER PRUNING.

have been cut away from the plants, these usually need little further pruning beyond removing weak growth near the base, and perhaps shortening a shoot or two to preserve the balance of the bushes. When the plants have been well protected, the strong growing sorts may be cut back to within 9 inches or 1 foot of the old wood, weak growers to within 2 to 4 inches. Often the frost does all the pruning that is needed.

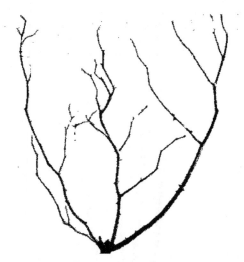

TEA ROSE BEFORE PRUNING.

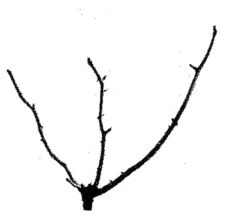

THE SAME PLANT AFTER PRUNING.

Pruning Newly Planted Roses

Q. Will you kindly say how and when I should prune climbing Roses planted in November ? — *P. M., Basingstoke.*

A. There are two courses open to you in pruning your climbing Roses which were planted in autumn. The third week in March you can shorten them either a little or much. Leaving the shoots nearly full length or half length you will doubtless get a certain number of blooms the first summer, but the plants will make unsatisfactory growth. If you cut down all the shoots on each plant to within 3 or 4 inches of the ground you will get no flowers from them the first year (or practically none), but they will make shoots 6 feet and

A SPLENDID PLANT OF ROSE RÊVE D'OR ON A COTTAGE FRONT FACING SOUTH, IN SOMERSET. THIS IS ONE OF THE BEST OF THE CLIMBING ROSES OF YELLOW SHADES.

more in length. These shoots will be vigorous and well ripened, will bloom profusely the next year, and will lay the foundation of a good plant.

Pruning Rambling Roses

Q. I have just (November) received some Rambler Roses from a nurseryman ; they all have four or five branches or shoots ranging from 3 to 5 feet long. After planting, should these be cut off, or left

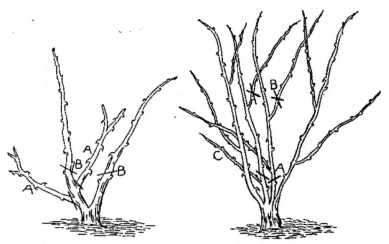

IN   PRUNING   ROSES   WEAK AND DEAD WOOD AS AT A IS FIRST CUT OUT. THE RE-MAINING SHOOTS ARE THEN PRUNED AS SHOWN AT B.

THINNING OUT A ROSE THAT IS   CROWDED   WITH   WEAK AND USELESS SHOOTS.   DO NOT PRUNE AT B, BUT CUT BACK TO A.

for the winter and pruned in the spring ? and when pruning, how much should be removed ? The names of the sorts are Lady Gay, Crimson Rambler, and Longworth Rambler. — *A. B. P., Southampton.*

A. If you have planted the Ramblers against some support, it will not be advisable to prune them until spring ; then cut back to within 3 or 4 inches of the ground. If planted out as free bushes cut back now to prevent swaying about in gales. Climbing and rambling Roses that are established are pruned as soon as the flowers are over. Pruning takes the form of cutting out some of the oldest growths—those that have bloomed. The finest flowers are produced on one year old shoots, *i.e.* those of the previous summer's growth.

Pruning Crimson Rambler Rose

Q. My plants of this Rose have made rampant growth. How do I prune them, and when ?—*Amateur, Feltham*.

A. It is best to thin out the old flowering growths as soon as they have finished flowering, and in the following March to shorten

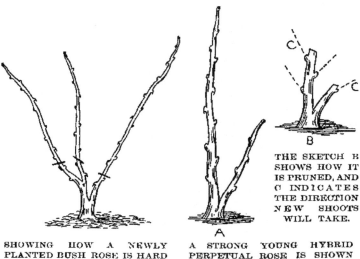

THE SKETCH B SHOWS HOW IT IS PRUNED, AND C INDICATES THE DIRECTION NEW SHOOTS WILL TAKE.

SHOWING HOW A NEWLY PLANTED BUSH ROSE IS HARD PRUNED.

A STRONG YOUNG HYBRID PERPETUAL ROSE IS SHOWN AT A.

the side growths. As your plant has made very little progress this season, all that can be recommended in the way of pruning is to cut clean to the base all thin, weakly growths, retaining the best. This should be done now (September).

Pruning Maréchal Niel Rose

Q. A Maréchal Niel Rose in my greenhouse has made vigorous shoots during the summer. How should these be pruned, and when ? —*Ignorant, Faversham*.

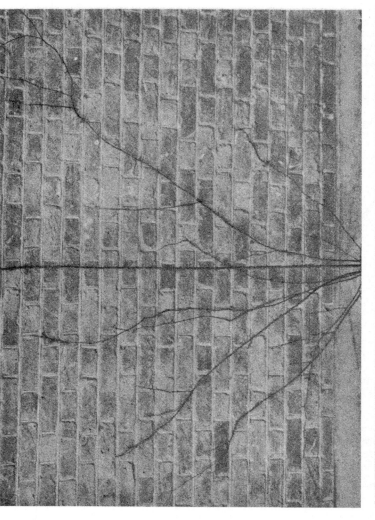

A PLANT OF CLIMBING ROSE, MADAME ALFRED CARRIÈRE (BLUSH WHITE) PLANTED IN MARCH, EVERY SHOOT BEING THEN CUT TO WITHIN 3 OR 4 INCHES OF THE GROUND. THE PHOTOGRAPH SHOWS THE ROSE IN THE FOLLOWING WINTER, SOME OF THE SHOOTS MADE DURING THE SUMMER WERE 6-8 FEET LONG.

A. The strong healthy growth made during the summer should not be pruned very much, if at all, for Maréchal Niel produces its flowers on the wood made the previous year. Hence to cut away this growth would mean the loss of many flowers in the coming season. The Rose should be well thinned of all weak shoots in winter, whether new or old, but the best of the past season's shoots should be retained and left as long as possible. Maréchal Niel is greatly benefited by summer pruning, say about the end of July or as soon as summer flowering is over. This consists of cutting back those shoots which have flowered to within 1 foot or so of their base. Young growths then develop, and it is these which, when well ripened, make the best flowering wood for the next season.

Roses That do not Droop

Q. Do any of the following Roses droop their heads when in bloom ? I have a Suzanne Marie Rodocanachi, which droops owing to the weight of the bloom, and I do not want any like that. Are the following as good as I can get in their respective colours? Capt. Hayward, Madame Ravary, General McArthur, Betty, Dean Hole, Madame A. Chatenay, Pharisaer, Prince de Bulgarie.—*Novice, Battersea.*

A. A few sorts that come nearly to your standard of perfection are Pharisaer, Princesse Mertchersky, Dean Hole, Lady Battersea, and Joseph Hill. Most of the varieties you name carry their blossoms erect, save Betty. This Rose is inclined to droop somewhat, but not to any extent.

Rose for North Wall

Q. Will you tell me what Rose I can plant on a wall with a cold north exposure ? It gets very little sun even in summer. Would a Gloire de Dijon do ?—*Fir Tree, N.B.*

A. You might plant any of the following : Gloire de Dijon (creamy yellow), Reine Marie Henriette (red), Félicité Perpétue (white), Bouquet d'Or (yellow shades).

Roses for Shady Wall 10 Feet High

Q. I have a wall 10 feet high which gets the sun about three hours in the afternoon. What Rose can I plant here ? I want one of good form and with high, pointed centre if possible, and, above all, free and continuous blooming. I am not particular as to colour, but should prefer a yellow. Bear in mind mine is a town garden. I also want to get five pillar Roses to give a succession of bloom, assorted colours and of good form. I already have Gloire de Dijon, Gruss an Teplitz, Lady Gay, and Crimson Rambler. Also a good white Rose. Would Madame A. Carrière suit me in this case? I should like to know why it is not advisable to buy bundles of Roses at auction sales.—*Anxious, Fulham.*

A. The variety of Rose that you would like for the 10-feet wall would be Kaiserin Friedrich or Bouquet d'Or. Either should grow in the somewhat shaded aspect, if you prepare a good deep hole for the roots. Five good pillar Roses would be Climbing Caroline Testout, Ards Rover, Conrad F. Meyer, J. B. Clark, François Crousse. Madame A. Carrière would be a splendid Rose for your proposed trellis. It is not specially beautiful in form, but is such a good grower that we could not recommend a better. A more perfect bloom would be Climbing K. A. Victoria, and we believe it would grow with you. Do not buy pot plants, but get good specimens from the open ground. They could be obtained for the price you name, 1s. 6d. each. We should not advise you to buy Roses at auction sales for the simple reason that you have to take what is given you, and usually they are the leavings after the season's sales. Moreover, the plants are allowed to stand about and the roots become parched up.

Six Roses for Exhibition

Q. Will you tell me the names of six Rose varieties for showing purposes?—*W. F., Nairn.*

A. You will find the following good, reliable sorts to grow. Dean Hole, Frau Karl Druschki, Mrs. John Laing, Mrs. W. J. Grant, Ulrich Brunner, Madame Jules Gravereaux. The latter is a very strong grower, but prune it down to the ground each year, and it will produce some enormous blooms.

Roses for Hedge

Q. I am anxious to plant a Rose hedge, and would be glad if you would tell me which of the following would be the most suitable. The hedge would be about 30 feet long, and unfortunately much exposed to north-west wind. Rosa rugosa, alba, rubra, Conrad F. Meyer, common Sweet Briar. Please suggest any more suitable, and give advice as to distance apart to plant, and pruning.—*A. S., Blackburn.*

A. If you desire a tall hedge, you could not do better than plant Conrad F. Meyer or the charming Penzance Briar Anne of Geierstein, which has rich crimson blossoms. But, possibly, as the hedge would

A PILLAR OF ROSE DOROTHY PERKINS. THIS IS A SPLENDID ROSE FOR BEGINNERS. HERE IS ITS CULTIVATION IN A NUT-SHELL. PLANT IN WELL DUG SOIL IN NOVEMBER; CUT DOWN TO WITHIN 6 INCHES OF BASE IN MARCH. IN SUCCEEDING YEARS CUT OUT A FEW OF THE OLDER GROWTHS AS SOON AS THEY HAVE BLOOMED.

be much exposed to west winds, you would prefer a hedge growing to about 5 feet high. This could be secured with Rosa rugosa, the red and white forms, and also mingled with them Blanc double de Courbet and Mrs. A. Waterer. The common Sweet Briar is deliciously fragrant, but you obtain little or no blossom. A Rose that makes a really beautiful and continuous flowering hedge is Gruss an Teplitz, a rich scarlet crimson sort and very sweet. If you cared to do so, you could blend a white Rose with it, *e.g.* Madame Alfred Carrière. The two are very free and continuous in their blossoming. Plant from 2 to 3 feet apart. In March cut the plants back to about 3 feet from the ground. If not so tall as this, do not prune at all. The second year cut down to ground one or more of the oldest growths, and repeat this every spring ; then you ensure a good base. Just a trim over will suffice for the other growths. Be careful to plant in well trenched soil in November.

Preparing Briar Stocks

Q. What will be the best mode of procedure in order to have a stock of rooted Briars for budding Roses on in summer — Tea Roses to be grown in pots ? Residing in a rural district, I have access to plenty of wild Briars to obtain cuttings. How shall I take them, and how must they be treated ?—*E. A. W., Somerset.*

A. Strong cuttings of the common Briar may be taken any time during September and October. Have them 9 inches long, and select only strong, well ripened wood ; cut close to a joint at the bottom, and remove all the buds except three at the top. Plant in rows 2 feet apart and 6 inches apart in the rows, burying the cuttings half their length or more in the ground, and press the soil very firmly about them. A mulch of leaf mould or old manure between the rows will be useful. They will hardly be strong enough for budding the next summer, unless strong cuttings are taken and they are watered in dry weather. The usual plan is to leave the cuttings one year to get well rooted. Transplant at wider intervals in autumn, and bud the next summer. There is not much gained by budding before the stocks are well rooted and strong.

Selection of Standard Roses

Q. Will you give a selection of eight Roses for standards, two pink, two red, two white, one yellow, and one other ? Wanted for garden decoration, good form, and sweet scented. Have already got The Bride, Joseph Hill, Madame Abel Chatenay, Hugh Dickson,

STANDARDS OF THAT FAVOURITE OLD PINK
ROSE, MRS. JOHN LAING (H.P.).

HYBRID PERPETUAL ROSE BARONESS ROTHSCHILD
GROWN AS A STANDARD, COLOUR LIGHT PINK.

Ulrich Brunner, Viscountess Folkestone, La France, and Général Jacqueminot. Would November planting be suitable for this district?—*S. B., London, S.E.*

A. The following have a good vigorous habit of growth, and are fragrant : Pink, Madame Jules Grolez, Gustav Grunerwald ; red, Commandant Félix Faure, Charles Lefebvre ; blush white, Augustine Guinoisseau, Clio ; yellow, Madame Ravary ; and Pharisaer, a good blush to make the eight. Plant in November.

Best Cream and Best Yellow Roses as Half Standards

Q. I should be glad to know of the best ten cream and yellow Roses to grow as half standards out of the following selection : Gloire Lyonnaise, Marie van Houtte, Florence Pemberton, Madame Falcot, Francisca Krüger, Madame Jules Gravereaux, Madame Hoste, Madame Ravary, Rubens, Madame Pernet Ducher, Madame Jean Dupuy, Madame Bérard, Dean Hole, Hon. Edith Gifford, Souvenir de Pierre Notting, White Maman Cochet.—*C. S. H. S., Shrewsbury.*

A. Of the list submitted we would recommend the following : Gloire Lyonnaise, Marie van Houtte, Madame Falcot, Florence Pemberton, Madame Jules Gravereaux, Madame Hoste, Madame Ravary, Madame Pernet Ducher, Souvenir de Pierre Notting, White Maman Cochet.

Twelve Roses for Cold Garden

Q. Would you give me the names of a dozen Roses, hardy and strong, for a cold garden ? The wind is keen. I have tried several dozen and find many weak ones fail.—*G. Bates, Derbyshire.*

A. The following varieties should grow well if you have the soil deeply dug : Conrad F. Meyer, Madame G. Bruant, Ulrich Brunner, Caroline Testout, H. Schultheis, John Hopper, Boule de Neige, Margaret Dickson, Dr. Andry, Gruss an Teplitz, Madame I. Periere, Augustine Guinoisseau.

Crimson Rose for Shady Spot

Q. Kindly give me the name of any crimson Rose other than Crimson Rambler that will grow in rather a shady place and quickly cover a fence 8 feet high.—*Bourne End.*

A. Either Hiawatha or Reine Olga de Wurtemberg would be the sort to plant for quick growth. The first named is perhaps the best and its lovely clusters of single flowers are always much admired.

ROSE LADY GAY IN A GARDEN IN THE SUBURBS.
THE SAME CULTURAL TREATMENT AS OUTLINED ON
PAGE 13 IS APPLICABLE.

Roses for Suburban Garden

Q. My garden is in a London suburb. I am anxious to take up Rose growing. Will you tell me how to prepare the ground, and give list of suitable varieties?—*Ealing.*

A. The trenching or double digging is carried out as follows in October : Mark out the soil to be trenched in 1-yard lengths, or if the borders are narrow, or the plot of ground a circular bed, the principle will apply, that is, to move the top soil to the depth of the spade, and with a five tined fork well fork up the lower soil to the depth of the fork. This soil is not brought to the surface, but kept where it is. All that is done is to mix some good manure with it. If you cannot procure farmyard or other good manure, then use basic slag at the rate of 8 oz. to 1 square yard. This material can be obtained of any horticultural sundriesman. Having put the lower soil right, add some bone meal to the top soil at the rate of about 3 lb. to a wheelbarrowful of soil. It will be all the better if the soil is allowed to settle down before planting, which should be done, if possible, by the middle of November. Be careful to choose fine weather for planting. Trim the roots fairly hard back and plant very firmly, treading the soil about them as tightly as possible, but leave the surface soil loose. A few good sorts to commence with are Caroline Testout, Hugh Dickson, Frau Karl Druschki, Gustav Grunerwald, Lady Ashtown, Mrs. John Laing, Madame Ravary, Prince de Bulgarie, Madame Jean Dupuy, General McArthur, Joseph Hill, and Viscountess Folkestone. If you have a spot where you could grow a good large bush plant Conrad F. Meyer, and should you desire one or two for arches or trellis we recommend Dorothy Perkins, Tausendschon, and Hiawatha.

Roses for Heavy Clay Soil

Q. What would you suggest as the best six or eight Roses suitable for a rather heavy clay soil? I prefer H.T.'s or Teas to H.P.'s, but would act as you suggest. Can you also tell me if you would recommend J. B. Clark as a good garden Rose? If not, the nearest H.T. to this colour.—*Phroso, Herts.*

A. Eight good Roses for your garden would be Caroline Testout, Frau Karl Druschki, Madame Jean Dupuy, Madame Jules Grolez, Prince de Bulgarie, Viscountess Folkestone, Marie Van Houtte, Laurent Carle. We cannot recommend J. B. Clark as a good garden Rose, although splendid at times. We much prefer Hugh Dickson. This is really the best crimson Rose for any garden.

CLIMBING ROSE MADAME D'ARBLAY (WHITE).

Roses with Long Pointed Blooms

Q. Would you be good enough to name half a dozen Roses for the garden that produce long, pointed blooms, double, and of good habit, etc. ?—*J. L., Cardiff.*

A. The following are excellent varieties possessing this qualifica-

BLOSSOMS OF THE EXQUISITE HYBRID TEA ROSE BETTY, SOFT
SHADES OF ROSE AND YELLOW. GOOD IN AUTUMN.

tion. Frau Karl Druschki, Lady Battersea, Pharisaer, Dean Hole, Madame Hoste, White Maman Cochet.

Sweet Scented Roses

Q. Please give the names of any Roses similar in colour to or better than Madame Abel Chatenay, and sweetly scented. Also the names of two or three very dark Roses that are scented, and suitable for growing in this neighbourhood.—*A. Saunders, Wimbledon.*

ROSE CONRAD F. MEYER, A VERY VIGOROUS AND VERY THORNY
JAPANESE BRIAR ROSE WITH LARGE AND FRAGRANT PINK BLOOMS.
A MAGNIFICENT ROSE. THRIVES IN HEAVY SOIL AND PARTIAL
SHADE. CUT OUT A FEW OF THE OLDER GROWTHS IN SEPTEMBER.

CRIMSON ROSES. HUGH DICKSON (TWO BLOOMS ON LEFT) AND GENERAL MCARTHUR. BOTH ARE VERY FRAGRANT AND GOOD IN AUTUMN.

A. Few if any Roses can compare with Madame Abel Chatenay as an all-round variety, but we can recommend the following as being really good and fragrant : Mrs. David Jardine, Madame Segond Weber, Elizabeth Barnes, Betty, Lyon Rose. The following very dark Roses are scented : Charles Lefebvre, Abel Carrière, Jubilee, Louis Van Houtte, Xavier Olibo, and Pierre Notting.

Bright Coloured Roses

Q. Kindly give me names of Roses—real good Hybrid Perpetuals —of the beautiful, full, deep colour of Duke of Wellington and A. K. Williams. I do not want bluish reds at all—just the pure deep glowing colour mentioned above. I have tried many of the so-called (catalogued) crimson and deep scarlet, but when they bloom they are often disappointing. Out of thirteen varieties—which I hoped from description to be near the same colour—only the above two pleased me.—*F. G., Bolton.*

A. You are asking for Roses that do not exist. We could name some brilliant colours, but they have no special beauty of form ; indeed, some are very thin. We do not know how you can find fault with such a superb Rose as Charles Lefebvre or Général Jacqueminot or Duchess of Bedford. Such Roses need to be established a year or two to see them in their real beauty, and you are expecting too much the first season after planting. A few sorts that we think will please you are Commandant Félix Faure, Comte Raimbaud, Hugh Dickson, Duke of Edinburgh, Duke of Teck, Thomas Mills, and from the H.T.'s Charles J. Grahame and General McArthur. François Crousse and Ards Rover are also two brilliant colours, but these are very vigorous, although they may be grown as free bushes.

Hybrid Tea Roses for Planting in Masses and for Show

Q. I enclose a list of dwarf H.T. Roses I have just marked, and should be glad to know if you think them a good lot for bedding, and also if suitable for local show. Mrs. W. J. Grant, Countess of Derby, Dean Hole, Earl of Warwick, H. Armytage Moore, Joseph Hill, Lady Ashtown, Laurent Carle, Madame Abel Chatenay, Madame Mélanie Soupert, Monsieur Paul Lédé, Mrs. D. McKee, Mrs. Harold Brocklebank, Richmond, W. E. Lippiatt, William Shean, Madame Hector Leuilliot (climber), Frau Philip Gedaldig. Is it possible to transplant successfully during November, Hybrid Tea, Roses (bush and standard) budded this summer on cutting Briar —*E. W. W., London Suburb.*

A. Yes ; these may be transplanted in November, and they will be tolerably successful, but we do not advise this being done if it can possibly be avoided, as you would obtain nothing like the vigour from the buds you would if the stocks were not disturbed. The list you give is a very good one, and you will not be far wrong in planting the varieties named. There are a few good show Roses which you might add, such as Mrs. Theodore Roosevelt, Madame Jules Gravereaux, Florence Pemberton, Madame Segond Weber, Lyon Rose, Princess Mertchersky, and Yvonne Vacherot, that would be immensely useful to you for exhibition purposes.

Roses for Pergola

Q. I have just put up a pergola in my garden in Hertfordshire, and should be glad to know of a good selection of varieties to plant. I want chiefly Roses that give good quality blooms.—*E. W. W.*

A. The selection given below, when established, cannot fail to make a very beautiful feature of the garden. For a pergola to look really well it is necessary that there should be a certain simultaneity of flowering of the various sorts planted. As you wish to confine your pergola to Roses we name a few fast growing sorts that should be planted at intervals, say of about 8 yards. For east side the following rapid growers are recommended, Dorothy Perkins, Hiawatha, Edmund Proust, White Dorothy Perkins, Blush Rambler, Delight. For the west side, Félicité Perpétue, Mrs. F. W. Flight, Crimson Rambler, Lady Godiva, Madame Alfred Carrière, Minnehaha. Plant about four varieties of the following in between each set of two fast growers in the order named herewith. For east side, Waltham Climber No. 1, Climbing Caroline Testout, Monsieur Desir, Climbing La France, Aimée Vibert, Conrad F. Meyer, Kaiserin Friedrich, J. B. Clark, Alister Stella Gray, Climbing Captain Christy, Ulrich Brunner, Madame Jules Siegfried, Reine Marie Henriette, Climbing Frau Karl Druschki, Rêve d'Or, Madame Wagram, Boule de Neige, Ella Gordon. On the west side, Gloire de Dijon, Gaston Chandon, Climbing K. A. Victoria, Climbing Mrs. W. J. Grant, Madame I. Periere, Crepuscule, Ards Rover, Nova Zembla, Madame Bérard, François Crousse, Climbing Devoniensis, Climbing Pride of Waltham, Zephirine Drouhin, Gloire Lyonnaise, Lady Waterlow, Duchesse d'Auerstadt, Hugh Dickson, Madame Hector Leuilliot, Dr. Rouges, Mrs. Paul. The above selection is made primarily with the object of providing a glorious show at one time, although they will give Roses throughout a long period.

Six Darkest Roses

Q. Please name the six darkest red Roses for the garden.— *W. E., Bishop Auckland.*

A. The following are good reliable sorts : Prince C. de Rohan, Abel Carrière, Louis Ricard, Baron de Bonstetten, W. E. Lippiatt, Charles Lefebvre.

ONE OF THE NEWER ROSES, H.T. MRS. SOPHIA NEATE, BLUSH, ORANGE ROSE IN CENTRE. VERY FINE IN BUD.

Roses for North Border

Q. I should be glad to know which are the best Roses to plant on a border facing north.—*Deborah, Berks.*

A. Most of the Rugosa or Japanese Roses would grow well on this border, and we can recommend the following : Conrad F. Meyer, grown as a pillar Rose ; Blanc double de Courbet, Madame

Georges Bruant, Mercedes, Rose à parfum de l'Hay, Mrs. Anthony Waterer, Chedane Guinoisseau, and the single pink and single white Rugosa for their lovely and showy fruit. The Penzance Briars would do well in this border, and the Hybrid Briar Una would be a beautiful object. Some of the Hybrid Chinese and Hybrid macrantha Roses, such as Chenedale, Charles Lawson, Paul Ricart, Lady Sarah Wilson, Mrs. O. G. Orpen, Lady Curzon would be fine, but let them be grown as pillar Roses, or if not, give them plenty of space, say 4 feet each way, so that they develop into good large bushes. The following would also make more variety : Magna Charta, Heinrich Schultheis, Boule de Neige, Clio, Madame Eugène Fremy, Cheshunt Hybrid, Gruss an Teplitz, Pink Rover, Crimson Globe (Moss), Celestial (Maiden's Blush), Madame Hardy (Damask).

Fragrant Climbing Roses for House Wall

Q. I want to plant a good climbing Rose, sweet scented, to cover a house wall that faces due south. The forecourt is of cement, but I have a hole some 2 by 1½ feet already made. What variety do you advise ? Shall I plant in November, and how shall I prepare the soil ? Also, I want a few quick climbers, sweet smelling if possible, to grow on poles at the back of bed 15 feet long facing due south ; what shall I get and how many ? I also want a few Roses to plant on a lawn facing north ; will you recommend a long flowering variety ? —E. W. H., Forest Gate.

A. In such a district as Forest Gate you require a good vigorous variety, and as you desire a sweet smelling Rose we think Gruss an Teplitz one of the best for your purpose. This is scarlet. If you prefer a creamy white, then plant Madame Alfred Carrière. Some good quick climbers for poles would be Hiawatha, René André, Blush Rambler, Dorothy Perkins, Conrad F. Meyer, Noella Nabonnand, Zephirine Drouhin. Some good perpetual flowering Roses to plant on lawn facing north would be Hugh Dickson, Mrs. John Laing, Ulrich Brunner, Mme. Abel Chatenay, Grace Darling, Gustav Gruner, wald, Madame Jules Grolez, Commandant Félix Faure, La France, Augustine Guinoisseau, Charles Lefebvre, Prince C. de Rohan, Senateur Vaisse.

Rambler Rose Dying Off

Q. Would you tell me the reason for a Crimson Rambler dying off ? The wood is going yellow and the leaves go yellow also and fall off. It was planted in clay on light soil against the root of an old dead Pear tree. I have other Ramblers in the garden which are doing well. I enclose one or two leaves.—*H. H. N., Hornsey.*

A. It may be that the plant has cankered at the junction where it was budded, but we think most probably the cause could be traced to its roots being in uncongenial soil of insufficient depth. We advise you to have a larger hole dug out in autumn, taking care that the soil is moved 3 feet deep and as much in width and breadth. In returning soil mix with it some good manure, and after the soil has lain for about two or three weeks replant your Rose, or, better still, procure a new one on its own roots. These Roses are readily procurable in this way now, and they are much superior to budded plants.

Roses Failing

Q. I enclose two cuttings of two different trees. Can you tell me the cause of their getting in this condition ? I planted twelve in a bed 6 feet square in March. The bed was a new one ; 2 feet of soil with 9 inches of stones under, and manure just below the roots, and well manured on top. All of the trees are in the same state more or less. I got the trees from a reputable firm. They have a fairly sunny aspect.—*E. D., Bolton.*

A. Your soil is probably too light for Roses, and you may have given the bed too much drainage. The specimen growths sent appeared as though the plants had been burnt up. Perhaps you did not plant them firmly enough. Roses need to be planted very firmly, and it is a good plan to go over the plantation a week afterwards and press the soil again with the heel. It may be the plants had been frozen at the root ere you received them, or perhaps you did not prune them. Rose plants should be cut back hard the first season after planting, to within 3 or 4 inches of the ground.

Climbing Roses Failing on West Wall

Q. On a wall facing west of a house I have recently taken there are three Rose trees trained, Crimson Rambler, Hiawatha, and Gloire de Dijon, the lower parts of which are nearly bare, and the remaining leaves all affected by apparently the same disease. I enclose specimens. Your advice would be esteemed.—*Rosey, Salisbury.*

A. All the Roses have suffered from red spider, a pest that frequently attacks wall Roses. Crimson Rambler is notoriously addicted to this when planted against a wall, the very worst position for it, and it has probably given it to the others. We should advise you to remove this Rose to the open garden in the autumn. Good syringing upon the under side of foliage will stop the pest as much as anything, and plain water should be frequently employed ; but at intervals of about ten days syringe with a solution of liver of sulphur made by dissolving 1 oz. of the sulphur in 10 gallons of water.

Roses on Wall Flowering at Top Only

Q. Roses planted against a wall have grown up immensely tall, and only have leaves and blooms high up, because there was a thick growth of other plants low down—*i.e.* up to 5 or 6 feet. These are now removed, and the long, bare stems of the Roses look very miserable. Had I better cut the Roses back and these bare stems, leaving them, say, 3 feet high ?—*M. de K., Essex.*

A. Cut down the oldest stems of the Roses to within 2 to 3 feet of the base in March. Bend down the remainder in a horizontal direction, fastening them to the wall. This should induce them to break into growth also near the base, after which you can cut off the tops. Give the plants a mulching of manure as soon as pruned.

Artificial Manures for Roses

Q. I am unable to obtain farmyard manure. What is the best artificial fertiliser to use ?—*E. J. K., Caterham.*

A. What is known as Tonks' manure is an excellent preparation, and should be applied in February at the rate of $\frac{1}{4}$ lb. to 1 square yard of surface. It is compounded as follows : Superphosphate of lime, 12 parts ; nitrate of potash, 10 parts ; sulphate of magnesia, 2 parts ; sulphate of iron, 1 part ; sulphate of lime, 8 parts. It should be well hoed in or lightly forked in.

Dried Blood as Manure

Q. I shall be glad to know whether, 1, this manure can be successfully used in the growth of Roses, and if so, whether, 2, it should be incorporated with the soil when trenching?—*Amateur, S. Wales.*

A. This is a very useful stimulant for all crops, but should only be applied during the growing season. Apply about 1 oz. to the square yard at intervals of two weeks, from May to July, forking or hoeing it into the surface soil.

Half-inch Bones for Roses

Q. Will you enlighten me on the following ? I have been told that if $\frac{1}{2}$-inch bones are mixed with the soil in which Roses are to be

A GATHERING OF PINK ROSES FROM A GARDEN IN THE SUBURBS. THEY INCLUDE MADAME JULES GROLEZ, GRACE DARLING, AND OTHERS.

planted, it makes them produce superabundance of roots and little
top. Also that it produces mildew, which works from the roots
upwards. Is this so?—*F. B., Ipswich.*

A. There is no truth in the assertion that bones are injurious to
Roses, in fact it is the other way about, as you may see if you turn
out a pot Rose in which bones have been mixed with the soil.
Every little rootlet will quickly lay hold of the small particles.
Half-inch bones are more durable for outside planting. We should
advise about 1½ lb. to 2 lb. to 2 bushels of soil, or say, two handfuls
for each plant, well mixing it with the soil. There should be farmyard manure applied at the same time if possible. Both standards
and Ramblers benefit by the application of ½-inch bones.

Basic Slag and Kainit for Roses

Q. I have been told that these are good for Roses, but am ignorant of the manner of using them. Can you help?—*Man of Kent.*

A. Basic slag, being nearly half free lime, would be an excellent
dressing for land rich in organic matter. The basic slag contains
from 16 to 18 per cent. of phosphoric acid, and the kainit about
12 per cent. of potash. Do not apply more than 8 oz. per square
yard of the basic slag, and 2 oz. to 3 oz. of kainit. The mixture
should be dug in as deeply as may be done without injury to the
roots, and the earlier in the winter this is done the better will be the
effect the following season. In the spring, where the basic slag and
kainit have been used in the winter, you may apply a dressing of
2 parts superphosphate and 1 part sulphate of ammonia, pointing the
mixture very lightly into the soil or hoeing it in, 2 oz. to 3 oz. being
applied per square yard.

Rambler Roses and Others from Cuttings

Q. Please tell me the correct time to take cuttings of Sweet Briar,
climbing Polyantha, and Wichuraiana Roses. What kind of shoots
should be taken? I am told that some Roses besides Gloire de
Dijon will flower with little or no sun. Could you kindly name
them? I have struck various Teas in water. Will the above kinds
answer thus?—*Enquirer, Shrewsbury.*

A. The best time to put in cuttings of the Rambler Roses and
other hardy kinds is early in October. Good, well ripened growths
are best. Those that have flowered the same year make up into
very good cuttings. You could first take off the laterals that bore
the blossom, if possible securing a heel or piece of the old wood, and

cut this through with a sharp knife. The cuttings should be about 8 inches in length. Sometimes these laterals will make two or three cuttings. Use the strongest wood you can get, providing it is not soft and pithy. Plant them in the open garden on a piece of well dug soil, and let the rows be about 12 inches apart, and the cuttings

IF CUTTINGS OF ROSES ARE INSERTED IN A FLOWER POT FILLED WITH SANDY SOIL IN LATE SUMMER OR EARLY AUTUMN, THEY WILL FORM ROOTS IN A FEW WEEKS IF PLACED UNDER A HANDLIGHT IN A GREENHOUSE.

about 4 inches apart in the rows. They should be put in almost their full depth, merely leaving about $\frac{1}{2}$ inch above the soil, and be careful to tread them in very tightly. It is a good plan to put a little sandy soil for the ends of cuttings to rest on. Most Roses prefer sunshine, but the Scotch Roses will grow in the shade, also the Rugosa or Japanese tribe. We should not advise you to strike

A ROSE CUTTING TWO MONTHS AFTER INSERTION. IT WAS TAKEN IN AUGUST AND TREATED AS DESCRIBED ON THE PREVIOUS PAGE. THE ROOTS MAY BE SEEN.

these Rambler Roses in water, as it would be too late in the year for
this method of rooting them. They would strike very well in water
the same as Tea Roses, but you would need to put the cuttings in
in July in the greenhouse.

Spraying Roses for Mildew

Q. My Roses are now (September) covered with mildew. What
can I do to cure them ?—*S. E. T., Reading.*

A. Towards the end of summer, when the leaves of Roses are
white with mildew, people are anxious to know what they can do to
check the disease ; but it is then too late to save the plants from
disfigurement. The white part seen on the leaves is the fruiting
stage of the fungus, which has already been on the plant for
a considerable period. If, however, preventive measures are taken
early in the year, the fungus does not obtain a firm footing. An excellent time to spray for mildew is early spring, just as growth is
commencing. The spraying ought to be done twice or thrice, at
intervals of a fortnight. Bordeaux mixture is one of the most
suitable preparations to use. It can be prepared as follows :
Dissolve 3 lb. of copper sulphate in warm water, placing the
mixture in a barrel holding 22 gallons. In another vessel slake
2 lb. of fresh burnt lime, and make to the consistency of a creamy
whitewash ; then strain through canvas into the barrel of sulphate
solution, make up to 22 gallons with water, stir well, and apply as a
fine spray to every part of the branches. If this spraying is per-
severed with, very little mildew will appear later in the year.

Climbing Roses for Unheated Greenhouse

Q. Please name the best six climbing Roses for small, sunny,
unheated greenhouse.—*H. E. J., Walthamstow.*

A. The following are six good climbers for this purpose ; Bouquet
d'Or, Cheshunt Hybrid, W. A. Richardson, François Crousse, Climbing C. Testout, Climbing Frau Karl Druschki.

Climbing Roses for Heated Greenhouse

Q. I am about to plant two climbing Roses in my conservatory to
cover the wall. The house is a leanto, facing north-east, the floor
bricked. Would it be best to take up a few bricks and plant in the
earth or plant in tubs ? The sorts I intend planting are Niphetos and
Maréchal Niel. Please tell me how to treat them.—*Scale, Witter-
sham.*

D

A. Unless you can prepare holes fully 3 feet deep and as much in width, and fill them with good soil, we should advise you to plant the two climbing Roses in tubs. Procure extra strong pot grown plants, and in transplanting be careful only to remove crocks and a little of the soil on the top edges. Soak the ball of soil in a bucket of water for a few minutes before planting. With these pot grown plants no pruning is needed the first year.

ROSE LITTLE PET GROWN IN A FLOWER POT.

Soil for Potting Roses

Q. Can I use ordinary soil from the garden borders for potting Roses?—*Enquirer, Blackheath.*

A. A potting soil for Roses should contain a fair amount of turfy soil. The garden soil sent is anything but this. It might be used in a small proportion with loam, otherwise we should not advise you to take much trouble in storing it. Try to procure the top spit from some pasture land, and stack this with alternate layers of cow manure; then in twelve months you will have some good compost in which you can grow some grand Roses.

Roses for Christmas

Q. I am about to build a greenhouse. What is the earliest time for Roses to flower, as I would like some for Christmas? Please name six best Roses for early forcing. Would pots be best for forcing Roses as I would like to use them?—*C. W. C., Warwick.*

A. Roses can be had in bloom by Christmas. The plants should be in pots and well established. Try your nurseryman for two year old plants that have not recently been repotted. These would give you the best results. Sometimes there are nursery sales where you could procure suitable plants. The six best sorts for early forcing would be Liberty, Madame Abel Chatenay, Richmond, Madame Ravary, Madame Hoste, Mrs. W. J. Grant. You must allow about three months between the starting of the Roses and

ROSE MME. N. LEVAVASSEUR (CRIMSON), AN EXCELLENT VARIETY FOR GROWING IN POTS IN THE GREENHOUSE.

their blossoming, therefore you should obtain the plants in September, and prune them lightly by the last week of that month.

Bush Roses in Pots

Q. Kindly inform me how to treat bush Roses in pots (just finished flowering in greenhouse) from now (May) up till the time of flowering in greenhouse next spring.—*G. H., Colchester.*

ROSE AENNCHEN MÜLLER (ROSE-PINK), AN ADMIRABLE ROSE FOR THE GREENHOUSE.

A. The plants that have just finished flowering should be placed outdoors on a bed of ashes, covering the pots with ashes up to the rim. Take care they do not become dry, and keep all flower buds pinched off. In September the plants should be repotted into a size larger pot if the pots are full of roots, but if not very well rooted merely top dress them. This is done by removing about 1 inch or so of the top soil, then sprinkling a little Clay's Fertilizer upon the soil, and filling up the space with fresh soil, such as good loam and well decayed manure in equal parts. Keep the plants outdoors on the ashes until November, then place them in a sheltered spot until Christmas. At this time they should be pruned, cutting back the current season's growths to three or four buds. The plants may then either be placed in the greenhouse or in a cold frame. If in the greenhouse commence with a temperature of about 45° at night, increasing to about 50° by day. As growths develop the temperature may be increased up to 65° by day, about 10° less by night.

Roses for Forcing

Q. I am anxious to have a few pot Roses in bloom in my greenhouse in spring. How do I proceed?—*H. E. S., Stourbridge.*

A. The best results are always obtained when the plants have been established in their pots a year, but plants from the open ground, if potted up early in October and placed at once in a cold frame, may be put into a gentle heat about February and will yield some very good blossoms. If you elect to do this you should make a selection from the Hybrid Perpetuals and Hybrid Teas, and for your guidance we would name the following as being suitable : Frau Karl Druschki, Caroline Testout, La France, Mrs. John Laing, Captain Hayward, Mrs. W. J. Grant, Liberty, Madame Ravary, Ulrich Brunner, and Duke of Wellington. Procure plants on the Briar, and when obtained trim over their roots a little and cut off all foliage, and reduce the length of the shoots to about 18 inches. A compost of 3 parts good loam, 1 part well decayed old manure, and some ½-inch bones, about 3 lb. to a barrowful of compost. Mix all well together and keep in an open rainproof shed. Use either 7- or 8-inch pots, and be careful to pot very firm. If weather is dry after potting give them a watering with a fine rose can and put plants on a bed of ashes in the frame, but keep the lights off night and day until frosts threaten.

Maréchal Niel Rose in Greenhouse

Q. In December I planted a Maréchal Niel Rose in greenhouse. This has made four strong shoots, one 12 feet long and three somewhat shorter ; these I have trained on separate wires about 6 inches from roof ; should the points of these be pinched out now (July)? There are also side shoots growing from these four ; should they be stopped? Kindly advise me.—*J. M. P., Southend.*

A. Your plant has made very good growth. As to what you cut away depends upon the condition of the growths. If well hardened only a few inches of extreme ends of all shoots need be removed, but if the shoots are soft and sappy then cut away 2 or 3 feet of each. There is yet time for the growths to ripen if you just pinch out the points and give as much air as possible, at the same time keep dry. About the early part of the year is soon enough for this Rose to start into new growth. Cut back the side or lateral growths in January to one or two eyes from main growth.

Various Roses in Town Greenhouse

Q. I have two glasshouses, one is a cold house 7 by 8 feet, and about 10 feet high, a leanto ; the glass comes to within 6 inches of the ground. I should like to grow some Roses in it. No Roses will grow outside. There is a disused chemical works at the back, I suppose that is the reason, and also being near the city.— A. K., Glasgow.

A. You are of course heavily handicapped in being near a large city and also near chemical works. Still you should be able to grow some good Roses in the cold greenhouse if you provide the plants with good soil to root into and afford them liquid manure in the growing season. Under glass there is always a tendency for the Hybrid Perpetual Roses to run to wood instead of flowering. You must check this by pruning very sparingly. Treat the plants more as pillar Roses or as climbers. You could easily put Bamboo canes about 5 to 6 feet high in the tubs and tie growths loosely to them, then in pruning merely shorten back to one or two eyes the side or lateral growths that eventually appear. Caroline Testout would be much more serviceable than Victor Hugo. Instead of J. B. Clark we would advise you to plant Hugh Dickson, and if you could find room for a yellow plant Madame Ravary, which gives such delightful buds.

CHAPTER II

Carnations in Winter and Summer

Perpetual Flowering Carnations Out of Doors

Q. Are perpetual flowering Carnations of any value for growing out of doors ?—*E. J. W., Hampton.*

A. Yes, they are invaluable. If put out in May they bloom all the summer, until October in fact. They are most accommodating. Plants that have flowered in the greenhouse throughout the winter will bloom out of doors the following summer, if planted out in May. They are put out in ground that has been well dug; they need no attention beyond watering during dry weather, staking and an occasional application of artificial manure, this being sprinkled round about the plants and hoed in.

Perpetual Flowering Carnations in Greenhouse

Q. Can one grow Perpetual Flowering Carnations in an unheated greenhouse ?—*X. Y. Z., Bude.*

A. No ; they need an average winter temperature of 55° ; that is to say that the thermometer must not fall below 45° in cold weather, while during sunny days it may rise to 60° or higher. When the latter temperature is reached a little air should be given.

Perpetual Flowering Carnations from Cuttings

Q. Is it difficult to raise them from cuttings ?—*Adrian, Swanage.*

A. No ; providing the material in which the cuttings are inserted is warmed. They are rooted most successfully in fine sand (silver sand is perhaps the best). Boxes some 3 or 4 inches deep are filled with sand, the cuttings are dibbled in and made as firm at the base as is possible. The boxes are then placed on the hot water pipes. It is wise to have the boxes prepared a few days before the cuttings are put in so that the sand may get warm. If the sand is watered before the cuttings are put in, probably little more will be required. However, the sand must not be allowed to get really dry. The best cuttings are those taken from towards the base of flowering stems. They are put in preferably during January, February and March, although they may be inserted until June. The box

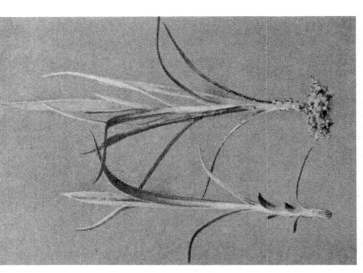

CUTTINGS OF WINTER FLOWERING CARNA-
TIONS FORM ROOTS QUICKLY IN SAND ALONE
IF THIS IS KEPT WARM BY BOTTOM HEAT.

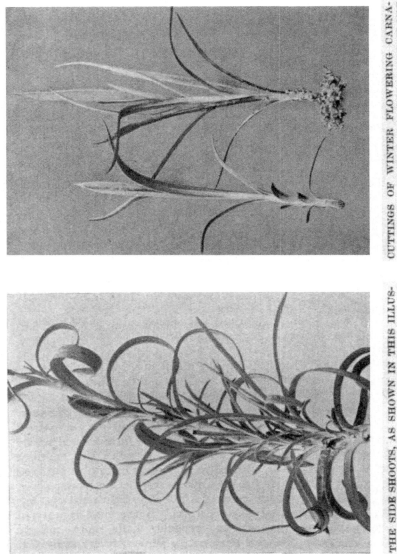

THE SIDE SHOOTS, AS SHOWN IN THIS ILLUS-
TRATION, MAKE THE BEST CUTTINGS AND
ROOT EASILY.

containing the cuttings is covered with a piece of glass ; this should be turned over every morning to allow the moisture that gathers to disperse.

About Tree or Perpetual Flowering Carnations

Q. Will you please advise me as to tree Carnations ? I received them in April, just out of thumb pots, the plants being 3 or 4 inches high. I potted into 60's in rich soil rather too tightly, I think, because the foliage grew somewhat crinkled. However, they got over that, and in July I potted on into 48's and 32's (according to the condition of the roots), this time in the Chrysanthemum compost with an extra liberal allowance of mortar rubbish, and ramming less hard than I do the Chrysanthemums. Some threw up stems for blooms, but these I pinched back close, and all are now (August) healthy and well on boards in the sun. The growths are 10 to 12 inches long, and pots full of roots. Kindly advise whether I shall be right to give similar treatment to that which usually suits Chrysanthemums. — *J. I. P., Lewisham.*

A. Yes; you should treat the plants as regards

WHEN THE CUTTINGS ARE WELL ROOTED AND POTTED OFF, THE TOP OF THE GROWTH IS PINCHED OUT TO INDUCE OTHER SHOOTS TO FORM.

potting and housing in the same way that is suitable for Chrysanthemums. But, of course, it is not advisable to ram down the compost too firmly. Some feeding will be necessary when the flower stems commence to run up. Leave space for top dressing. You were rather late in potting; the final potting should be done in June. It is a mistake to stop the shoots at the time of potting.

Winter Carnations

Q. How should Perpetual Flowering Carnations be grown so as to provide flowers from October until April ?—*J. J., Bristol.*

A. Briefly, this is the method of treatment. Cuttings are inserted in January as already described. They will be rooted in 6 weeks. They are then potted in small pots, turfy soil with plenty of sand intermixed, being used. It is wise to give little or no air for a week afterwards, so as to help the plants to root quickly in the fresh soil. The plants are kept in the greenhouse until early May. They are then put out of doors, or else in a cold frame; the latter is preferable, because heavy rains can be kept off. They need all the fresh air possible. The pots are plunged to the rims in ashes, whether the plants are out of doors or in a frame. They must be given larger pots as they need it, or in other words as soon as well rooted. It is usual to repot in April, and again finally in June, flower-pots of 6 or 7 inches diameter being used on the latter occasion. Use a soil mixture of turfy soil 2 parts, and old manure, such as that from a mushroom bed, 1 part. Failing this, use 1 part soot and ½ inch bones, 3 parts turfy soil. In September the plants are brought into the greenhouse and will begin to bloom in October. Probably no fire heat will be necessary at first to maintain a night temperature of 45° to 50°. The question of "stopping" or pinching out the points of the young shoots is an important matter: the object is to make the plants bushy. The first stopping becomes necessary in April when the plants are potted for the second time. The top of the little plant is pinched out, only some five joints being left. Several shoots will develop. These must also be stopped when about 3 inches long. Stopping the shoots should cease at the end of July. It is most important to keep the soil moist throughout the summer: this is accomplished by watering thoroughly where the soil appears to be getting dry. During the winter the plants need far less water than in summer, but the soil must still be kept moist; an occasional sprinkling of fertiliser should be given, say every three weeks.

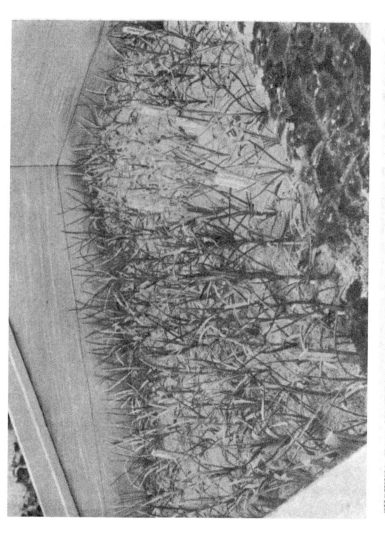

SHOWING HOW CUTTINGS OF PERPETUAL FLOWERING CARNATIONS ARE INSERTED IN SAND UNDER A FRAME IN WARM GREENHOUSE.

Twelve Good Perpetual Carnations

Q. Can you give the names of 12 good varieties ?—*Anxious, Birmingham.*

A. New sorts are being brought out every year now. The following are some of the best of those in commerce : Britannia, red ; Enchantress, pink ; Afterglow, rosy-cerise ; Jessica, white with red marking ; Mrs. Burnett, salmon-pink ; Rose Pink Enchantress, rose-pink ; Winsor, silvery-pink ; Victory, scarlet ; White Perfection, a beautiful white ; Royal Purple, purple ; Mrs. Lawson, cerise-pink ; Harlowarden, dark crimson ; Black Chief, dark crimson ; Aurora, buff shade.

Preparing Beds for Border Carnations

Q. I am about to buy a collection of good varieties of Carnations. How should I prepare the ground for them ?—*Nemo., Brighton.*

A. In order that this plant may bear up well in a hot, dry season, the soil should be dug deeply. As your soil has only six inches of good soil and thin clay below, we should advise you to have the ground dug 18 inches deep, taking care that the clay is kept at the bottom. A layer of manure should be put in the bottom and another layer 6 or 8 inches below the surface. Having so trenched the land you could then mark out the paths and put the soil on top of beds. You must look out for wireworm, as this pest is very prevalent in old pastures. Give the soil a dressing of Vaporite or Kilogrub as you plant. We think for this season we should keep the plants in their pots during the winter, seeing that the soil is not ready. When the soil is prepared in good time then we prefer to plant out the rooted layers in October. A cold frame is a good place to keep the plants, and they are not afraid of cold and some frost. Keep the lights well tilted during wet weather ; in fact, the hardier they are brought up the better. A little lime added to the soil when trenching would be an advantage. Well rotted manure is best to use. A dressing of well rotted manure to the surface after planting is very helpful.

Best Scarlet Border Carnation

Q. Please say which is the best Scarlet Carnation.—*W. P., Romford.*

A. The best Scarlet Carnation is Cardinal (Douglas). There is another one of this name. Twelve good Carnations for amateurs : Agnes Sorrel, Benbow, Charles Martel, Cardinal, Daffodil, Helen

Countess of Radnor, John Pope, Lara, Miss Ellis, Miss Willmott, Trojan.

Border Carnations from Cuttings

Q. Will you please tell me if it is possible to grow Border Carnations from cuttings?—*E. D. S., Swansea.*

CARNATION ELIZABETH SHIFFNER (ORANGE-YELLOW),
THE FINEST NEW BORDER CARNATION.

A. Some people like to root border Carnations, and especially the Clove section, from cuttings, and October is the time to begin. They may be inserted in a sandy compost either in pots or boxes and after being watered should be placed for the winter in a cold frame, which, being kept always close, preserves the leaves from flagging. Many of the Pinks also may be rooted in the same manner, the best cuttings being those broken off with a heel—piece of old stem. Mule Pinks should be treated similarly ; some of these, of which Napoleon III. may be mentioned, require to be renewed annually from cuttings.

Twenty-four Carnations that are Really Fragrant

Q. So many Border Carnations are scentless, that I should be glad to learn of two dozen really fragrant sorts.—*Helen, Derby.*

A. Mr. James Douglas recommends the following as being fragrant varieties : Agnes Sorrel, Banshee, Beauty, Bella Donna, Bertie, Boadicea, Burn Pink, Castilian, Charm, Chloris, Countess of Paris, Cupid, Enid, Floradora, Helen Countess of Radnor, H. J. Cutbush, Mr. W. Incledon, Much the Miller, Narses, Pink Beauty, Queen of Scots, R. Berkeley, Tantallon, Twilight.

Best 12 Self and Fancy Carnations and 12 Picotees

Q. I should be glad to know which you consider to be the best 12 Self-coloured Carnations, the best 12 Fancy Carnations, and the best 12 Picotees ?—*E. O. W., Bexley.*

A. Self-coloured Carnations : Daffodil, W. H. Parton, Cassandra, Miss Shiffner, Sir Bevys, Hildegarde, Isinglass, Benbow, Lady Hermione, Miss Willmot, Mrs. E. Hambro', Francis Samuelson. Fancies : Argosy, Horsa, Monarch, Liberté, Lady Ardilaun, Merlin, Ivo Sebright, Richness, Yeoman, Professor Cooper, Banshee, Rony Buchanan. Picotees : Dalkeith, Mrs. W. Heriot, Hesperia, Childe Harold, Duchess of Roxburghe, Lady St. Oswald, Gronow, The Pilgrim, Lauzan, Daniel Defoe, Gertrude, Amy Robsart.

Carnation Attacked by Eelworm

Q. Will you kindly hold a post mortem on enclosed corpse of Carnation, and announce result ? The flower stalk looked gouty.— *S. M. K., Sutton.*

A. The portion of stem was swarming with stem eelworm (Tylenchus devastatrix) and its eggs. The full grown eelworm is about $\frac{1}{25}$ inch long, and in appearance resembles a tiny eel, with both ends pointed, the hind end specially so. The refuse of infested plants should be burned, and the place whence they have been uprooted, in the case of Carnations, soaked with a solution of formalin (formaldehyde 40 per cent.), 1 fluid oz. to 5 pints of water, in order to destroy the pests in the immediate vicinity of the diseased root, as well as where it has been. After this treatment, and in the course of a fortnight or three weeks, the ground may be dressed with basic slag and 6 oz. of kainit per square yard, forking into the ground about 6 inches deep, and leaving until February, then fork over the ground a spit (10 to 12 inches) deep, breaking up well. Shortly afterwards, and before sowing seeds or setting plants, apply a top dressing, to be lightly pointed or raked in, of a mixture of 2 parts superphosphate and 1 part sulphate of ammonia, applying 2 lb. of the mixture per rod, or 2 oz. per square yard. As a further precaution against eelworm and other ground pests, the ground may be dressed with Vaporite.

Diseases that attack Carnations

Q. Can you give me a few notes on such diseases as commonly attack Carnations, together with preventives and remedies?—*H. T. J., Hereford.*

A. Several diseases cause sad work with Carnations, particularly mildew, green fly, eelworm, wireworm, spot disease of the leaves, and earwigs. If your plants are grown indoors a great deal may be done to prevent disease by giving suitable cultural conditions. A rather dry atmosphere is required, with free ventilation without draughts. Mildew may be kept in check by dusting affected plants with sulphur. In the case of spot disease the worst of the leaves should be removed and burnt, and the remainder dusted with sulphur. Plants that are very badly affected ought to be burnt; plants affected by eelworms ought also to be burnt. Green fly may be kept in check indoors by fumigating, and outdoors by syringing with soft soap water into every 3 gallons of which ½ pint of paraffin has been well mixed. Wireworms often cause serious injury by boring through stems and roots. They may be caught by trapping with pieces of Carrot or Potato placed 1 inch or so beneath the surface. These traps ought to be examined each morning and the wireworms destroyed. Earwigs may be trapped by placing small pots partly filled with dry moss amongst the plants. Earwigs will get in amongst the moss for shelter, and may be caught and destroyed.

CHAPTER III

Sweet Pea Difficulties Made Clear

Selection of Sweet Peas

Q. Please say how you would improve on the following collection of Sweet Peas, most of which I have already got. 1, Zephyr ; 2, Crimson Paradise ; 3, Evelyn Hemus ; 4, Paradise Ivory ; 5, Paradise Carmine ; 6, Constance Oliver ; 7, Elsie Herbert ; 8, Olive Ruffell ; 9, Mrs. Charles Foster ; 10, Helen Paradise ; 11, Gladys Burt ; 12, Edna Unwin ; 13, Clara Curtis ; 14, Arthur Unwin ; 15, Masterpiece : 16, George North Improved ; 17, Mrs. H. Bell ; 18, Etta Dyke; 19, Marjorie Willis ; 20, Syeira Lee.—*R. G., Ellon.*

A. The list of varieties is a strong one. I should add Douglas Unwin or Prince of Asturias for a maroon ; Mrs. Hardcastle Sykes or Princess Victoria for a blush ; The Marquis or Tennant Spencer for mauve ; and Helen Pierce for a veined blue. These will make up two dozen.

Manure for Sweet Peas

Q. I have prepared 2-feet trenches for growing Sweet Peas next year, and have mixed with the soil, which is fairly rich, a good supply of $\frac{1}{4}$-inch bones. In my yard I have a well which receives the drainings from the stables of six horses. Would the sediment and the liquid be safe applied now (November)? And what quantity should be used? Would you advise letting it remain on the ground until spring or digging in at the time applied? Would the result from this be equal to stable or cow manure?—*H. J. F., Portsmouth.*

A. On the whole the ground would benefit by the contents of the well ; the only drawback is that it may tend to make the soil slimy. If you have left the ground rough and lumpy you may safely put the stuff on direct, otherwise you should mix it with ashes before applying it. You might put it on 2 inches thick. Leave it on the surface before turning it in. It could hardly be so good as stable manure, because it would produce less humus ; still, it has got to be disposed of somehow. The best plan of all would be to use it on ground to be planted with Greens, and employ stable manure and chemicals for the Sweet Peas.

Sweet Pea Buds Falling

Q. I wonder if you can tell me what causes my Sweet Pea buds to fall off just as they are coming out. The plants look perfectly healthy, but all the first flowers have been taken in this way, leaving the stalk on just as if the buds had been picked off. I enclose you some stalks, one of which has a bud just falling.—*S. J., Oxted.*

A. The earliest buds often fall, and little anxiety need be felt as the later ones are not affected. The cold wet weather of which we have had so much this summer is no doubt responsible for the flowers falling. If you have been overdosing them with manure the buds would naturally fall.

Preparing Ground for Sweet Peas

Q. I wish to grow Sweet Peas on ground which is of a very heavy nature ; about 18 inches down there is a kind of blue clay, which is sticky when wet—it is like cutting soap. I propose going down about 2 feet, putting in road grit and manure, mixing well. Should I be doing right in incorporating with the manure, etc., basic slag, or would lime do as well ? If so, in what proportions should I use either, or both ? Should kainit and lime be applied when preparing ground, or is it best to put on top of ground and hoe it in after trenches are filled ?—*In Doubt, Enfield.*

A. Do not bring the clayey subsoil to the surface, but thoroughly break it up and leave it below. Apply the basic slag at the rate of 4 oz. per square yard and mix it with the soil about 9 inches below the surface. Apply lime at the rate of 8 oz. per square yard, and put it on the surface. Both should be applied in the autumn, but the lime one month after the basic slag. Four ounces of kainit per square yard may be mixed with the latter and applied at the same time.

About Stopping Sweet Peas

· *Q.* Is there any advantage in snipping off the tops of Sweet Pea plants when a few inches high ?—*Doubtful, Harrow.*

A. When Sweet Peas grow to the height of about 3 inches and are then stopped, it has the effect of making the plants break out from the base. Thus the Sweet Peas become bushy, producing more growths from the base than would otherwise be the case. Pinching back, provided it is not carried out to excess, also induces an increased formation of roots, which is an advantage, especially to floriferous plants like Sweet Peas. Plants which have been pinched

E

do not ultimately attain the same height as plants which are not stopped, that is providing other conditions are equal. At the same time, if the plants are stopped once only in their lifetime the difference in height is not very great. This method is chiefly advisable with weakly plants.

Growing Sweet Peas in pots

Q. Please give concise directions for growing Sweet Peas in pots to bloom from April to June.—*E. W. S., Southen?.*

THIS SWEET PEA IS OF THE VARIETY DOROTHY ECKFORD, AND WAS GROWN FROM ONE SEED SOWN IN A MIDLAND GARDEN.

WELL GROWN SWEET PEAS IN A GARDEN IN NORFOLK.

A. Seeds are sown in September, 5 or 6 seeds round the edge of a 5 inch wide flower pot. Keep in a cold frame until December, then bring in greenhouse. Temperature should not exceed 50° without sunheat. Neither should it fall below 40° in cold weather. Use a fairly light soil, turfy soil two thirds, leaf soil and sand one third. In January the plants will be only about 6 inches high, but with a little sunshine they will grow rapidly, being by then well rooted. Keep the soil fairly moist. More water will be needed as growth becomes more vigorous. Give a little air when the thermometer registers 55° under the influence of sunshine. Occasional applications of Clay's Fertilizer much diluted may be given from March onwards.

Sweet Peas Killed by Pea Mould

Q. Can you tell me what is the matter with the Sweet Peas I send you ? They have been quite a failure.—*E. O. H., Walsall.*

A. The plants are quite dead at the roots, reduced to the condition of thin rusty wire, and the leaves are all dried up, browned, and more or less dead. They have been destroyed by the Pea mould (Peronospora trifoliorum var. viciae). Wet weather favours the fungus. With better weather the plants should improve, as the fungus is not only an early affection, but is also retarded by fine dry weather. The plants may possibly be benefited by watering with a solution of iron sulphate, ½ oz. to 1 gallon of water, using this along both sides of the row, but not over the plants, and if these have the rootstems sound it is likely they may recruit, otherwise there is very little hope of betterment. You may use the sulphate of iron solution once a week, and as a general fertiliser for Sweet Peas a solution containing ½ oz. each of superphosphate of lime and kainit (high quality), and ¼ oz. each of nitrate of soda and iron sulphate to 4 gallons of water. Of course, this must not be used where the iron sulphate solution is employed, and it is advisable to alternate this with lime water, adding a tablespoonful of soot to each gallon of lime, forming the soot into a paste previously so that it can be readily mixed. All the diseased plants, as they go off, should be pulled up and burned, not leaving any part of the haulm in the ground, not even portions of leaves.

Sweet Peas in Same Spot Year after Year

Q. My garden is so small that I shall be compelled to grow Sweet Peas in the same place year after year. How am I to treat the soil? Will any system of manuring be successful, or must I have fresh soil for each crop?—*C. L. S., Surrey*.

A. It is advisable, though not really necessary, to remove a portion of the soil and replace it with fresh. Trench the ground 3 feet deep, and put in some well rotted manure, and also a dressing of superphosphate at the rate of 4 oz. per square yard. The plants would derive much benefit from a dressing of superphosphate at the rate of 2 oz. per yard run of row while they are growing. Keep the powder from the haulm.

Pig Manure for Sweet Peas

Q. Will you be so good as to give me your opinion of pig manure for Sweet Peas? I am digging my trenches now (November) 4 feet deep, and propose putting the pig manure under the bottom spit. The soil is 15 inches light top soil and fine sand underneath, no gravel or clay at all. Will lime be of any use in this soil, besides superphosphate of lime?—*R. C., Surrey*.

A. Yes; you may mix the pig manure freely with the soil about 10 inches below the surface. Do not use lime now, but apply superphosphate of lime at the rate of 2 oz. per yard run of row, when the plants are growing freely. Commence in April and give applications every twenty days or so.

CHAPTER IV

Flower Garden Trials and Troubles

How to Destroy Worms on a Lawn

Q. Will you please tell me if there is any possible way of ridding a bowling green of worms, or of stopping them from lifting the surface in the autumn ?— *W. W., Reading.*

A. You may place 1 peck of lime in 20 gallons of water and stir the mixture well. Then allow it to settle and add another 20 gallons of water. When the liquid has once more settled and is clear, water the lawn with it through a fine rosed watering-can. The worms will come to the surface, when they may be swept up. Apply in autumn and spring.

Quantity of Lawn Seed to Sow

Q. Can you tell me how much lawn seed to sow for a lawn of 600 square yards.—*H. J. E., Harrow.*

A. The usual quantity of lawn seed to sow is about 40 lb. to 50 lb. per acre. To sow 600 square yards would therefore need about 5 lb. or 6 lb. of seed. Providing your ground is well prepared and level, the seed might be sown at any time now (March). Choose a quiet day when there is little or no wind to carry the seed about at the time of sowing, and be sure that you obtain good lawn seed from a reliable nurseryman. Sow across from north to south and from east to west.

Weeds on Lawn

Q. Will you kindly advise me the best way to eradicate a weed from my lawn ? This starts with small plants, and finally becomes quite a large patch, and these patches are now spreading considerably. The weeds grow so close that little if any grass grows through hem.—*F. N. Hulton, East Sheen.*

A. Lawn sand will destroy Daisies on lawn, and would destroy this (Plaintain). This is the cheapest and simplest way we know of getting rid of such weeds. It must be applied in spring, just before the grass begins to grow. It may be had of all seed merchants and sundriesmen, with directions how to use. It has the effect of turning the grass brown for a time, but it quickly recovers. Or you might dig up the roots with an old knife, and if necessary sow fresh seed.

How to Look After a Lawn

Q. I have recently sown down a lawn. Please give me a few hints on how to attend to it during the season.—*M. T. E., Hampstead.*

A. Protecting the seeds until they have taken root is important, for if left unprotected birds will destroy more than half of them. Black thread stretched across the ground helps to keep them away. The young grass as soon as it starts grows rapidly at this time of the year (April), and at the end of three weeks after sowing it will have made sufficient progress to be safe from further molestation. Other means adopted for keeping birds away are netting, and setting up scarecrows with old clothes, etc. The young grass should be rolled as soon as it has attained the height of 2 inches. This consolidates the soil round the roots, and causes them to spread more freely. For the first three times the young grass is best cut with a scythe. It should be cut the first time as soon as it is 6 inches long and afterwards every three weeks, when for the rest of the season the lawn mower may be used, but the knives of the machine must not be set lower than ½ inch from the surface for the first month, and not at any time to cut so low as to injure the heart of the young grass plants. If all has gone on well, the lawn may be lightly used for play at the end of the summer, but it would be better to defer doing so until the following season. Should the spring and summer prove to be exceptionally dry, the grass, especially in the early stages of growth, should receive copious waterings.

Renovating the Lawn

Q. Is the present (October) a good time to set about improving a lawn. If so, what should be done?—*Anxious, Stockport.*

A. One may do a great deal towards ensuring a good sward by attending to the lawn in the autumn. Now that the lawn mower may almost be discontinued, large weeds should be dug out, the holes filled with soil, and the lawn well rolled—indeed, rolling in the autumn has a very beneficial effect, as it keeps the worms down and makes the green firm. Late in the autumn is the time to spread over the grass a light dressing of old manure and soot. It may not be very sightly, but it does improve the grass, and one can afford to put up with a little unsightliness during the winter months

Improving Neglected Lawn

Q. Would you tell me what I can do with a lawn which has been so neglected that the greater part consists of Plaintains. To root them up looks an endless task.—*Box, Wallingford.*

A. The best and most economical method of restoring a lawn is to feed it every autumn or spring time. Turf requires food like all other kinds of plant. Use the remains of a Cucumber bed or, better still, well rotted manure. Have it finely sifted and mixed with loam or soil, and give the turf a dressing of 2 lb. to the square yard. To repeat the quantity in February or March will do good. Plaintains can be removed by sulphuric acid, 1 drop to the crown of each weed ; but as it is destructive of other than vegetable matter it must be confined in a bottle, allowing only 1 drop to escape.

Moss On Walks

Q. The walks in my garden are covered with moss. What is the best way to get rid of it ?—*E. J. K., Wallingford.*

A. The best way to destroy moss on gravel walks is to dig the gravel over, burying the moss in the bottom. Lay the gravel in the best position to throw off the water, and roll it down firmly. If the walk cannot be turned, sprinkle salt over the surface in sufficient quantity to give it a white appearance, picking a dry time for the work ; or use one of the advertised weed killers, mixed in the way advised by the manufacturers. Moss is often troublesome owing to the dampness of the soil ; and when this is the case nothing short of draining the spot will permanently get over the difficulty.

Top Dressing a Lawn

Q. My lawn is thin and the grass does not seem to flourish. Would a top dressing of manure improve it ? if so, when should this be applied ?—*Lawn, Herts.*

A. The best time for doing this is the late autumn ; the early part of November will be found suitable. It would be far better to apply a mixture of half rotted short manure, together with an equal bulk of old potting soil and a bag of soot, than to apply soot as a dressing alone, for we note that the soil is chiefly sand and is lacking in substance. Let the dressing be applied evenly all over the surface to the depth of about 1 inch, and use about half as much soot as potting soil. Leave the dressing to be washed in by the rains. In late January or February the dressing should be repeated.

When to Put down Weed Killer

Q. Will you advise me which is the best time of the year to put down weed killer for the destruction of weeds on paths and drives —in the spring, when they begin to grow, or in the autumn or winter ?—*A. B., Saxmundham.*

A. The weed killer will have a more lasting effect if applied in

THE BEAUTIFUL PALE BLUE DELPHINIUM BELLADONNA THAT COMES TRUE FROM SEED. HEIGHT ABOUT 4 FEET.

spring. If applied in autumn or in winter, the winter rains will have the effect of washing away its poisonous properties, making it easier for weeds to make an early growth again than would be the case if applied in spring.

Improving Lawn

Q. 1, how can I improve my grass plot and when should I do it ? It is very heavy ; the wet weather has made it very pasty, and it is almost impossible to walk on it now (November). Appears to have been laid on the heavy clay subsoil without proper (if any) drainage, has been neglected for many months. As I am only a tenant here for a short period, to take up the turf, drain the soil, and relay are out of the question. 2, what is the enclosed weed? and how can I eradicate it from the grass?—*W. J. P., Hornsey.*

A. 1, the best thing you can do is to put on a good dressing of gritty soil, such as road drift, during the autumn and winter months. Two dressings will be sufficient. 2, the weed you enclose is a Buttercup (Ranunculus), and the best way of getting rid of it is to put a few drops of oil of vitriol in the centre of each plant, or pull up every one, and as their habit is spreading this is a difficult matter. The vitriol is poisonous, and gloves should be worn when using the liquid. The latter may be dropped on the plants from a notched stick.

Time to Apply Basic Slag

Q. When is the best time to apply basic slag and how much should be given?—*Ignorant, Shrewsbury.*

A. This is a slow acting manure, rich in phosphates. It should be applied in the autumn, since it is some time before it is rendered available as plant food. The finer basic slag is ground the more valuable will it prove as a manure. It is not so valuable as superphosphate for vegetables, but it is a most suitable manure for lawns.

Making Brick Paths

Q. I should very much like to alter the paths in my garden and make them brick paved. Would it be possible for me to do it myself? Are new or old bricks to be used? Is mortar or cement of any kind required?—*M. I. B., Surrey.*

A. It is necessary to have a perfectly level foundation for laying bricks to form a path, and they must be cemented or concreted down, and the cracks where they join filled with the same substance. There should be a layer of cinders beneath the bricks some 2 or 3 inches thick to keep the path dry. The only plan for you to follow would be to find a working bricklayer, request him to supply you with good hard red bricks and the necessary binding material, and pay him a trifle for showing you how to do the work yourself. Now is a good time for the operation before frosts come. You could place the bricks say one third or half an inch apart, fill the cracks with sandy soil and put Violet Cress, Mentha and other tiny plants there.

IN AN IRIS GARDEN.

Violets in Frame in Winter

Q. Please tell me how to provide for a supply of Violets during winter.—*X. Y. Z., Reading.*

A. Make up a hotbed, half manure and half leaves, and put in the frame early in September. Upon this place 8 inches of soil; turfy soil 2 parts, leafy soil 1 part. There must be enough manure

A DELL OF FORGET-ME-NOTS.

put in to bring the plants within 2 inches of the glass. Fill the frame with manure and leaves, then tread it firmly, this will be about right. Plant the Violets ten days or so afterwards. Put them 10 inches apart. Keep the frame closed for a few days to encourage them to form fresh roots. Subsequently give air on every favourable occasion. They will not bloom if the frame is kept closed. Artificial heat is an advantage, because by this means frost is easily kept out, and the atmosphere made dry. Good varieties are Marie Louise and Lady Hume Campbell.

How to Grow Violets

Q. Will you tell me when to plant Violets?—*E. M., Swansea.*

SPRING FLOWERS IN A YORKSHIRE GARDEN.

A. The best time to plant is during April. The best plants to buy are rooted runners. A border should be prepared by digging and mixing with the soil well rotted manure and leaf soil. It is not advisable to have the border in a shady spot as is often advised; the plants should get several hours' sunshine. Plant the weak growing doubles 8 inches, and the strong growing single sorts 10 to 12 inches apart. They need little further attention during the summer months. Give water in dry weather and a dressing of manure to keep the border cool and moist. In August runners or growths will appear; these must be cut off. By September the plants will have formed good clumps; towards the end of that month is the best time for planting Violets in frames for winter flowering. The frame should be in a sunny position. Violets are most successful when grown fresh annually. Some of the single sorts do pretty well if left alone for two or three years, but most sorts thrive best if fresh beds from rooted offshoots are planted every April. Princess of Wales, Princess Beatrice and Czar are among the best of the large blue-flowered singles. Marie Louise is a good double, lavender coloured; Lady Hume Campbell, lavender blue; Comte de Brazza, white, and Mlle. B. Barron, blue, are other good double sorts.

Best Plants for Shady Border

Q. The best plants for a shady border with rather heavy, moist soil.—*G. K., Kent.*

A. Anemone Japonica and varieties, Kniphofia (Tritoma), Liliums candidum, Martagon, and croceum, Senecios clivorum and Veitchianum, Primulas Japonica and denticulata, Aquilegia (Columbine), Sedum spectabile, Foxgloves, Primroses, and Violets, hardy ferns in variety.

Plants for Dry Border

Q. The best plants for a dry border under trees.—*S. T. M., Oxford.*

A. Solomon's Seal, Hypericum calycinum, Doronicum Plantagineum, Lychnis coronaria, Funkia Sieboldii, Saponaria officinalis flore pleno, Foxgloves, Periwinkle (Vinca).

Plants for Warm Wall

Q. I have a brick wall, 2 feet 6 inches wide, 10 feet high, side of bay window facing south, now occupied by Virginian Creeper Could I train Ivy Geranium or Solanum in place?—*R. T. T., Fulham.*

A. You must take out every bit of root of the Virginian Creeper, then dig a hole 2 or 3 feet square, and fill with a mixture of the soil taken out, fresh turfy soil, a few shovels of decayed manure, and some coarse sand. Make it firm, and leave for a week to settle before planting. Neither Ivy-leaved Geranium nor Solanum is hardy, and would most probably die in winter unless thoroughly protected. The best plant for your purpose is Ceanothus Gloire de Versailles, a climbing shrub with beautiful blue flowers in August.

How to Preserve Buds and Flowers

Q. Can you tell me if there is anything I can do to preserve flowers after they are cut?—*J. K., Wimbledon.*

A. The following method of preserving flower buds so that they will bloom long after they are picked from the plant will interest you. Gather the buds when nearly ready to open, and seal up the ends of the stalks with sealing wax, wrap the buds in tissue paper, and put them in a tin box perfectly airtight. When the bud is wanted to open, cut off the sealing wax and put the stalk in water to which a little saltpetre has been added. The flowers can thus be had in bloom a month or two later than their usual season. I have tried the plan with Roses only, but I am told it is equally satisfactory with other flowers.

To prevent Butterflies depositing their Eggs

Q. Can you tell me if there is anything I can do to prevent the large white Cabbage butterfly from depositing eggs, and so to some extent rid my garden of caterpillars?—*A. E. W., Derby.*

A. The eggs of the large white butterfly are laid in clusters beneath the leaves, but the eggs of the small white, and also of the green veined white, are laid singly. This is important, as the eggs of the first are easily destroyed by looking for them as soon as the butterflies are noticed, and the pieces of leaves covered with them torn off and burned. This method will not answer for the small white or green veined white's eggs. You should have the chrysalids searched for and destroyed. These are chiefly found in outhouses, potting sheds, and like places under eaves or palings, or under pieces of rough timber. This can be done in winter time, and again in June or July when the first brood has pupated, the butterflies you recently saw being of that generation. Another means of reducing their numbers is to procure some strips of tin, and as many sticks pointed at one end for thrusting into the ground, cleft at the top, and so long as to be well above the Cabbages. Affix the sticks about 6 feet apart, smear the tin on both sides with a mixture of resin and sweet oil, two thirds of the former melted, and one third of the latter, and insert this in the cleft of the stick, one for each. The butterflies resting on the strips of smeared tin become affixed.

Value of House Slops

Q. Are house slops of any value in the garden?—G. E. S., Bucks.

A. If diluted with twice or three times as much water they form a valuable manure for such plants as Roses, Dahlias, and all kinds of herbaceous plants grown in borders. However, we do not advocate their use for pot plants.

Hardy Flowers for Early August

Q. I want to have my border gay in early August. What should I plant?— W. F., Newcastle-on-Tyne.

A. In your part of North Britain you would require varieties that blossom about the third week in the south of England. You will find the following very good. Phloxes : Coquelicot, Fiancée, Beranger, and Le Mahdi ; Monkshood (Aconitum Napellus bicolor), Anemone Japonica rosea and alba, Anthemis sulphurea, Aquilegias of sorts, Asclepias tuberosa, Aster Bessarabicus, Plume Poppy (Bocconia cordata), Bellflower, Campanula persicaefolia Moerheimi, Cephalaria Alpina, Chrysanthemum maximum King Edward VII., Chelone barbata, Coreopsis grandiflora, Gaillardia grandiflora, Delphiniums of sorts, Echinops ritro, Geum Heldreichii, Sunflower (Helianthus rigidus), Heuchera sanguinea, Inula Hookerii, Lychnis chalcedonica fl. pl., Papaver pilosum, Jacob's Ladder (Polemonium Richardsoni), Rudbeckia laciniata plena, Scabiosa Caucasica, Statice latifolia, Gypsophila paniculata, Torch Lily (Kniphofia corallina Pfitzerii).

Making a Small Pond

Q. I should be very glad of directions as to the making of a small pond in my garden.—H. S., Woking.

A. You should excavate the soil to the required depth and then puddle the bottom and sides with clay, the layer of clay being at least 4 inches thick. An edging of stones fixed with cement would look best, the stones being irregular in shape. Yes ; an amateur should be able to do the work. As you intend to allow ducks to go on the pond, plants as an edging would not answer well. The excavation of the soil would cost 6d. per cubic yard, but the cost of the carting, clay, stones, cement, and other work would depend largely upon local charges and facilities for obtaining material.

Flowering Plants for Heavy Soil

Q. My garden soil is clayey and very wet in winter. Many plants do not thrive. Can you give me a list of suitable sorts ?—*J. A. B., Southall.*

A. It is more than probable that the real fault of your garden lies in its being badly drained. One row or two rows of drainpipes placed about 2 feet below the surface, with a gradual fall to a proper outlet, would almost certainly improve the nature of your garden soil. There are certain flowering plants which thrive fairly well in a soil such as yours. Thus in addition to Irises and Montbretias, both of which flourish in your garden, you might try Sunflowers, Heleniums, Delphiniums, Trollius, Michaelmas Daisies, Hollyhocks, Lupins, and Aconite. There are several ornamental and flowering shrubs that would also give a good account of themselves ; for instance, Wistaria, Clematis, and Lonicera for pergolas and arches, Lilac, Laburnum, and Flowering Currant in the shrubbery. The application of quicklime when the ground is vacant tends to lighten a soil ; fresh or green manure from the farmyard should be avoided, as it increases the tenacity of a heavy clay. Long strawy manure, however, helps to lighten and aërate the soil by means of the small channels made by the long straw.

A Common Disease of Aster

Q. Please tell me what is the matter with the enclosed Asters. I shall probably lose all I have through this disease.—*E. A. T., Stockport.*

A. The plants are affected by the disease popularly known as blackleg, the roots dying and the rootstem turning brown and then black, and this extending to parts above ground. The plants become stunted, cease growing, and die. This has been attributed to various causes, such as attack by a white worm, called the Aster worm (Enchytraeus parvulus), but there is no evidence of this pest in your examples. The disease is of a fungoid nature and a close ally of the sleeping disease of Tomatoes and other plants. Resting spores remain dormant for a season, then germinate, forming a mycelium capable of attacking the rootlets of Asters. By this mycelium only can the plants be attacked, all attempts to inoculate above ground portions of the plant being futile. It is suggested to dress the ground with quicklime at the rate of $\frac{1}{2}$ lb. per square yard, slaking and mixing well with the soil, sprinkling on the turned up surface 2 oz. of kainit, leaving for the rain to wash

F

in. This is preferably done in autumn, and in early spring, before cropping again, the ground is forked over and a dressing of steamed bone meal applied, breaking up and mixing well.

Wallflowers Not a Success

Q. Can you tell me why my Wallflowers are not a success? I give them ordinary, careful treatment.—*Disappointed, Shrewsbury.*

A. Exceptionally firm planting is needed by this plant, which can

HARDY CYCLAMEN GROWING AMONG FERNS.

be seen flourishing on old walls where there would seem to be little root hold. Half the Wallflowers that turn yellow and die in gardens do so because winds have loosened them in the soil ; directly they become ill insect pests fasten upon them, and so wireworms and other creatures are generally blamed for the mischief that was first wrought by a careless gardener. Rich soil is needed for growing fine flowers ; it is a customary error to plant Wallflowers in dry, stony, unnourished ground just because they are known to live on walls. If any gardener will examine wall specimens he will not find them with large, lustrous foliage and immense richly coloured blooms, such as we now demand from the bed and border specimens —unless they have been especially cared for in their lofty nooks.

GLOBE FLOWERS (TROLLIUS EUROPAEUS) THRIVE WELL IN SHADE. THEY BLOOM IN MAY.

The Best Bedding Geranium

Q. I wish to have a blaze of colour in one bed and prefer to plant Geraniums. Which is the best variety?—*Hopeful, Chester.*

A. Zonal Pelargonium Paul Crampel is described as richest fiery scarlet in colour, with large flowers and trusses and fine foliage. A truer description was never given of a Zonal Pelargonium. Amateurs who have not yet grown this variety in their flower beds should do so. To obtain the best effect it is best to allow each plant ample space to grow in, and, if possible, to devote one large bed to them rather than mix them with other varieties. As a rule Zonals should not be planted in a rich soil; but the soil may be rich for Paul Crampel. It will then grow luxuriantly and produce trusses of flowers as large as the crown of one's hat.

How to Grow the Flame Nasturtium

Q. Will you please tell me the best way to grow Tropæolum speciosum? Ought I to start with seeds or plants?—*C. F., Colyton.*

A. You will have the greatest chance of success with this lovely flower if you obtain rhizomes, or underground stems, which are thick and fleshy, and somewhat like those of the bindweed in genera appearance. These ought to be planted 2 to 3 inches deep in fairly good, moist, loamy soil, in a north, north-west, or west aspect. Plant in autumn or spring. In some gardens it grows like a weed, whilst in others it is most difficult to establish. There is really no accounting for its perverseness sometimes, for if the conditions under which it thrives excellently in other places are apparently copied in every detail it fails to succeed.

Staking Perennials and Berried Shrubs for Wall

Q. What is the best way to stake hardy perennials 3 to 4 feet high to maintain a natural appearance and afford protection from high winds? What are the best berry bearing shrubs suitable for walls? also in the form of bushes for beds or borders?—*A. S., Brixton Hill.*

A. There are two ways open to you in staking your perennials. One method is to tie four or five stakes round each clump and run several rows of string round them. The other is to thin out the shoots well, then stake each one separately, taking care to insert the stakes so as to give each plant its natural position. The best evergreen wall shrubs are Crataegus Pyracantha, C. crenulata, Cotoneaster microphylla, C. buxifolia, and C. angustifolia. For borders all

SUCCESSFUL PLANTING OF A WALL IN A SUBURBAN
GARDEN.

the above may be grown except Cotoneaster angustifolia, whilst in addition Pernettya mucronata and Arbutus Unedo for a large growing shrub may be included.

Making a Window Box

Q. I am anxious to make a few window boxes. Can you tell me how to proceed ?—*Ellen, S. Wales.*

A. Window boxes may be made in a variety of designs and with many different materials. Small branches of unpeeled Larch are very useful and effective for covering the fronts of boxes. They can be arranged in diamond or star patterns, or simply nailed on vertically, with the ends rounded. Virgin cork can be used in the same way, sawing it carefully when working out designs with it, and breaking it up roughly when making a box with a simple rustic covering. More elaborate and fanciful boxes are made by using hearth or paving tiles, and enclosing them within a border of wooden moulding or wrought iron-work. Be sure to make holes for drainage in the bottom of the box, and put a strip of wood at each end of the box to keep the latter from contact with the window sill.

Should Gladiolus Bulbs be Lifted?

Q. Is it wise or necessary to lift Gladiolus bulbs every autumn and store them during winter ?—*W. M., Stafford.*

A. Only a few Gladioli, principally natives of Europe and Asia Minor, are quite hardy in the greater portion of the British Isles. The others are best treated as half hardy subjects, that is, the bulbs should be lifted in the autumn when the leaves become yellow throughout. Store them in a cool place where the frost cannot reach them until late March or early April, when they should be planted out.

Carnations and Dahlias for Exhibition

Q. I should be glad of a selection of first class varieties of Carnations and Dahlias that have figured prominently at recent shows. —*Carnation, Lancs.*

A. The following Carnations and Picotees are selected from the best stands shown at recent exhibitions : *Carnations*—Sir Galahad and Mrs. Eric Hambro, white ; Seagull, blush ; Daffodil, yellow ; Carmania, pink ; Bonnie Dundee, scarlet ; W. H. Parton, deep crimson ; Cantor, purple. *Picotees*—Miss Evelyn Cartwright, light red edge ; Lady Douglas Galton and Togo, yellow ground; Amy

Robsart, heavy purple edge ; Carrie Goodfellow, scarlet edge. The
Dahlias which follow are arranged according to the average number
of times they have been staged at the National Dahlia Society's
exhibitions held in recent years. Six Cactus Dahlias—J. B. Riding,
J. H. Jackson, Pearl, Mrs. Edward Mawley, Florence M. Stredwick,
and Nelson. Four Show or Fancy Dahlias—R. T. Rawlings, Mrs.
Gladstone, John Walker, and Duchess of York. This year's novelty

PAEONY FLOWERED DAHLIAS.

Tom Jones, is also worthy of a place. Four Pompons—Bacchus,
Nerissa, Tommy Keith, and Darkest of All.

Forty of the Best Cactus Dahlias

Q. I enclose a list of Dahlias (grown this year) which, thanks to
The Gardener, I have been very successful with, and would be very
pleased if you would kindly correct the list so as to represent forty
of the best Dahlias up to date. Alpha, Beacon, Britannia, Columbia,
Coronation, Cloth of Silver, Cockatoo, Dainty, Daisy, Daisy Easton,
Flag of Truce, F. M. Stredwick, Fairy, Harbour Lights, H. W. Sillem,

Hyacinth, H. Shoesmith, J. H. Jackson, J. B. Riding, Kathleen
Bryant, Lord of Manor, Manxman, Mrs. Grinstead, Mrs. Castleton,
Mrs. Wilkinson, Mrs. McMillan, Primrose, Pilot, Pearl, Pink Pearl,
Pink Perfection, Purple Jackson, Rev. A. Hall, Red Rover, Star,
T. Parkin, T. G. Baker, Victorian, Wm. Marshall, White Swan.—
J. B., Aintree.

A. Your list is a fairly comprehensive one, and includes practically all the older sorts worth growing. In weeding out the inferior
sorts, we should recommend omitting the following : Alpha, Beacon,
Dainty, Red Rover, Fairy, Coronation, Manxman, Pearl, Pink
Perfection, Daisy, Britannia, and Pink Pearl, and in place of these
add Snowdon, white; Rev. Jamieson, pink; Saxonia, crimson;
Brigadier, bright crimson; Monarch, bronzy red; Harold Peerman,
yellow; Mercury, yellow striped crimson; C. E. Wilkins, salmon,
pink; Flame, scarlet; Ivernia, fawn; Helium, yellow and orange;
and Nelly Riding, crimson tipped white. This would bring your
collection right up to date. We might, however, point out that for
garden decoration only some of the sorts discarded are very useful
but we take it exhibiting is your chief aim.

Failure with Tufted Pansies

Q. I should be glad of a few hints as to the cultivation of these,
I seem to have little success with them. They appear to be
attacked by some disease.—*B. S. K., Lincoln.*

A. In October or November the plants may be lifted and
divided. In dividing, each portion should have a few young growths
and some roots ; place them in rows 6 inches apart and 3 inches from
plant to plant in any convenient ground of a friable soil. Dust
lightly with air slaked lime and soot to keep down slugs and other
predatory pests. The plants can be lifted carefully in early spring,
say February or as soon as the weather permits afterwards, and
placed in the flowering quarters. This procedure gives opportunities
for manuring and preparing the ground for their reception. Those
plants that have turned quite yellow in the leaf and appear to
be dead at the roots, should be cleared away and burned, removing
as much of the rootstem as possible. It is evident that they are
infested by the Viola mould. The fungus is tided over winter
by resting spores in the rootstems of the diseased and dead plants,
hence the need for their removal. They should not occupy the same
ground again for a year at least. The ground where the collapsed
plants have been should be given a dressing of basic slag, 1 lb. per

TUFTED PANSIES OR VIOLAS. PHOTOGRAPHED IN MAY. THE PLANTS WERE PUT OUT IN AUTUMN.

square yard, and 6 oz. of kainit, digging in about 6 inches deep. Leave the soil rough during winter, and in February fork over a spit deep, mixing and breaking up well by taking small spits.

Plants for Bank

Q. My house is one of a terrace facing south-east, on high ground facing the sea. In front is a stiff bank, the soil of which is shallow. Nothing has grown there yet but weeds. Could you recommend or suggest an economical way of laying it out? It is too stiff for grass,

CROCUSES IN THE GRASS.

as I could not use a mower. I have thought of dwarf shrubs or Ice Plant.—*T. H. W., Dover.*

A. You could cover your bank effectively, and at the same time make it so that it could be easily kept at little or no after cost, by planting groups of various free growing shrubs, such as double Gorse, French Gorse, Cornish Heath, Ling, Heather, Lavender, Cistuses, Rock Roses (Helianthemums), Cotton Lavender, and Genista pilosa. Plant large irregular shaped masses of each in such a manner that the different sorts of things run one into the other, in a natural manner. Such a method of planting forms one of the very best kinds of wild gardening, for an ugly bank can be made effective during the whole of the year, and gives exceedingly little trouble when the plants are once established. You could, of course, use Ice Plants (Mesembryanthemums), but the other things would have the best appearance. If you desired it, a few flowering trees could be introduced if the position is not too wind swept.

Hardy Flowers for Sunny Border

Q. Can you suggest hardy perennials for a sunny dry border backed with a 3 feet wall? Border faces south, but gets some shade from a large Pear tree. From the rough plan I enclose, you will see I have Hollyhocks next the wall, then a gap of 2 feet at present planted with Canterbury Bells, and some bedding plants in front. I propose putting Brompton Stocks in the gap this autumn, but want

HARDY PRIMULAS IN A GARDEN IN THE NORTH OF ENGLAND.

to put other plants as well in between to flower later. I want them to be about 3 feet high to hide unsightly stalks of Hollyhocks. White Phlox would look well, but in such a hot position would not last any time. I do not care for yellow as it clashes so with bedding plants. I thought of Gypsophila, which does well here, with perhaps a few Phloxes in between. Is there a flowering shrub that would do in such a border as mine ? Also would you be good enough to tell me how you increase Gypsophila and when is the time to do it ? I buy small roots. The first year they do not do much, but the second they are 1 yard across. Our soil is light but good.—*To and Fro, Kent.*

A. Certainly Gypsophila would do well in such a position, but Phlox requires a very moist soil, and unless you can plant in a sunk bed and flood them well in summer we should advise you to omit these plants. Some of the large flowered Ox-eye Daisies, such as Chrysanthemum maximum M. Prichard, would be fine. Achillea The Pearl is a fine showy plant. Hydrangea paniculata would be very beautiful, so also would Philadelphus Lemoinei erectus, which flowers earlier than the Hydrangea. Then there are some of the white flowered hardy Chrysanthemums such as Belle Chatelaine, and white flowered Michaelmas Daisies such as polyphyllus. Aster vimineus is also a charming small flowered plant. You can increase Gypsophila paniculata by seed or cuttings. Sow the seeds in March and transplant the seedlings.

Pruning White Jessamine

Q. There is a White Jessamine covering an arbour in my garden. It is a thicket of growth. How should I prune it ?—*W. J. C., Wimbledon.*

A. You may allow a few main branches to remain almost their full length to form a base from which the flowering branches will spring. The secondary branches may then be cut well back during winter to within 1 foot or even less, say two or three buds, of the base of the previous year's shoots. The mass of branches which usually form at the base of such plants should be cut away each year, as they never flower satisfactorily and only serve to weaken the plant. Do not allow too many main branches to remain, or they will choke the plant up. The object should be to let as much sunlight and air as possible have free access to all parts of the plant.

Making the most of a Garden Frame

Q. I have a garden frame. How can I use it to the best advantage ? —*M. M., Worthing.*

A. The frame comes in very useful for salads, Strawberries, etc., early in the season. It may also be usefully employed to grow Cucumbers in during summer. I have wintered Cauliflowers,

Lettuce, and Calceolarias, protected Strawberries intended for forcing, hardened off bedding plants, and still had a good crop of summer Cucumbers out of the same pit, and with very little trouble indeed. Half hardy and deciduous ferns, and plants intended for forcing, may be wintered therein with safety by simply throwing a few mats over the lights at night and during sharp weather ; while in the early spring a crop of early Potatoes and Radishes may be had, and these may be got out early enough for growing Cucumbers and for ordinary propagating purposes. For raising seeds not requiring bottom heat I have found them of the greatest service—in fact, a cold frame need never be empty at any period of the year. From March until the end of May they may be occupied in hardening off Celery, Dahlias and other bedding plants, and from that time until the month of September by crops of Cucumbers and Melons, and in bringing on such subjects as Fuchsias, Petunias, Pelargoniums, Balsams, etc. ; from September till spring comes round again they may be filled with Cauliflowers, Calceolarias, and Strawberries that are intended for forcing purposes, and may be used for protecting winter salads, or anything of a half hardy nature.

Bulbs for Early Flowering

Q. Can you tell me which are the most suitable bulbs for forcing into bloom quite early, so as to have flowers to cut, say, in January.— *E. T. W., Hendon.*

A. For ease in culture and forcing into flower the amateur will find Roman Hyacinths and the Paper White Narcissi the best bulbs to secure. Pot in August and September. Bunch flowered Narcissi are useful when good bulbs are secured, but we have never found them give such satisfaction in a general way as do the Paper Whites. Place Roman Hyacinths as close together as they will go in 5- to 6-inch pots, and the Narcissi may well go into those 7 and 8 inches in diameter. Boxes can, of course, be used for both kinds of bulb, but these are more suitable for the large grower than the amateur with perhaps, one small house and a frame or two. Early Tulips of the Van Thol section may be secured and potted in September ; these are small and not in such favour as are the larger flowering sorts, but they are bright and, on account of their early flowering tendency, extremely useful.

Montbretias not Flowering

Q. I cannot understand how it is that my Montbretias do not bloom regularly. They are in good soil.—*Amateur, Southampton.*

A. Almost every year we hear complaints regarding Montbretias failing to bloom, and questions as to the cause of this. In at least nine cases out of ten this reluctance to bloom can be traced to similar causes. The mistake is made of leaving the bulbs in one position year after year, and as they increase so rapidly the soil becomes impoverished, the result being inevitable—little or no bloom. But if they are lifted, divided, and replanted about every three years, very different results will be obtained. Choose the sunniest position possible.

About Anemones

Q. The best soil, position, and time to plant Anemones.—*G. E., Surrey.*

A. The Anemones about which, we presume, you require information are the Poppy Anemone (A. coronaria), the Scarlet Windflower (A. fulgens), and the St. Brigid varieties. The position must be a sunny one, the best time to plant is September and October, although it may be done as late as the end of January. They thrive in well drained, light sandy soils, which should be freely manured. A mulching of leaf mould is very beneficial early in the year. Plant the roots about 3 inches deep, and 4 to 6 inches apart according to size.

Keeping Dahlias Through the Winter

Q. Can you tell me how to keep Dahlias through the winter ?— *Alpha, Bermondsey.*

A. Do not cut the plants down until the frost has well blackened them, and sever them about 1 foot above the ground, attaching the label of each securely to the stem. The lifting of the roots should be very carefully performed, using a fork. Do not be particular about removing too much soil ; it affords little protection to the tubers. The roots should be thoroughly dry before storing, but this must not be accomplished by artificial means ; if there is no sun place them in a cool, airy position, free from damp, and in a day or so they should be ready for their winter quarters. A dry, frostproof cellar is the best position for them, but those not possessed of this accommodation will find a cupboard or some similar place answer the purpose quite well, so long as it is dry, cool, and frostproof. During winter an occasional examination is necessary to remove any roots that may by chance have decayed.

CHAPTER V

The Greenhouse Gay

To Kill Green Fly in Greenhouse

Q. I have a greenhouse 9 by 5 feet, and I am removing into it about thirty Chrysanthemums—Japanese and incurved varieties. I want to fumigate them with the XL ALL vaporising compound, in the liquid (I suppose this is one of the best preparations for green fly, etc. ?) and should be glad to know how much liquid would be required to fumigate them. Would it in any way injure the flowers if they were in bloom when it was done ?—*Constant Reader, Ulverston.*

A. Yes; if you use XL ALL vaporising compound according to the instructions given with it, all the insect pests will be killed. Place the lamp on the ground near the centre of the house. A dessertspoonful would not be sufficient, but a tablespoonful would. Keep the ventilators closed all night, opening them the following morning. If not successful the first night use the compound again the following night. If the flowers are dry they will not be damaged.

Fern Fronds Turning White

Q. I enclose a fern frond. Could you tell me what is the reason for its turning white like that ? I have several varieties of this fern, and they all are attacked by insects.—*H. T., Macclesfield.*

A. The reason for your fern fronds turning white, as you describe, is that they are covered with the small insect known to gardeners as thrips. The insect is known scientifically as Heliothrips adonidum, and feeds on almost any kind of plants. The insects are usually most prevalent on plants that are growing in a temperature that is too high and an atmosphere that is too dry for them, and a bad attack is a serious matter and denotes bad culture. Your best plan is to cut away all the worst of the fronds, and burn them. Then dip the plants in an insecticide, such as Fir tree oil mixture or a nicotine mixture, several days running, and well fumigate the house once a fortnight for the next two months. Lower the temperature, keep the house well damped down and the plants well syringed, and you will soon see an improvement.

79

Heating Apparatus for Small Greenhouse

Q. I should be glad of your advice as to the best method of heating my greenhouse.— *W. X. Y., Rutland.*

A. Small oil stoves are very cheap, and fairly effective in keeping out frost; but they require very careful attention, else the fumes would be injurious to your plants. A small boiler (tenant's fixture), such as the Loughborough or Invincible, would be the most satisfactory for you in every way. Such a boiler costs about £2 10s., and

CUTTINGS OF TUFTED PANSIES.   ONE BAD CUTTING ON THE
LEFT, THREE GOOD ON THE RIGHT.

the pipes are not expensive. These boilers are fixed in the wall of the house, are fed from the outside, and the chimney is also outside. They maintain a good, steady heat, and are quite safe and most efficient.

Maidenhair Fern in Winter

Q. Can I keep Maidenhair Ferns nice and green throughout the winter? and if so, what do they require?—*X. Y. Z., London.*

A. Yes; you can keep your ferns green throughout the winter, for it is not natural for them to die down. You do not say whether you have got them in a greenhouse or dwelling room. If they are in a greenhouse a minimum temperature of 45° to 50° Fah. and a maximum of 50° to 55° should be kept. The pots should be stood on a cool ash or pebble bottomed stage, and the stage and floors of the house should be damped down twice a day, to keep the atmosphere moist. Do not let the plants become dry, but at the same time be careful not to over water them ; they will not require more than half the water they did in summer. About once every ten days give a little weak manure water if the pots are well filled with roots, but

WELL GROWN HYDRANGEA PLANTS, TWO YEARS OLD.

not otherwise. Keep a sharp look out for insects, and if thrips appear fumigate lightly two or three nights running. If in a dwelling room, much the same treatment will be necessary ; keep out of draughts, and in the event of cold nights stand the plants away from the windows.

Hydrangeas not Flowering

Q. I have about 500 Hydrangeas in 5-inch pots ; for some reason they did not flower this spring. They have been outside since June, the wood now (September) being well ripened. I want to get them in flower by the middle of May next. Will you kindly say when to cut down and subsequent treatment ?—*H. P., Appleby.*

G

A. As the wood is well ripened you should plunge the pots in ashes or tree leaves during the winter, and then put the plants in warmth in spring, in order to get flowers by the middle of May. If you can spare a cool frame, put the plants in it, and protect them only from frosts. It will not be necessary to cut down the plants really, but to lengthen the flowering period you may cut down some of them to good basal buds when you place them in heat in the new year. Feed liberally when the flower buds commence to develop.

Keeping Pansy Cuttings through the Winter

Q. I wish to know if the cuttings from Pansies will keep during the winter in an attic, and if so, should I cover with anything to protect from cold ? I do not possess a greenhouse.—*C. I. W., Kent.*

A. It is not necessary to put Pansies in either a greenhouse or attic in order to keep them through the winter. If subjected to such treatment the plants would be greatly weakened. Make up a nice bed-in the garden, and grow the young plants there. If very severe weather comes fix a few arched sticks in the border and then put mats on them.

Cineraria and Calceolaria during Winter

Q. Can I keep these plants during the winter without artificial heat ?—*Enthusiast, Doncaster.*

A. The Calceolarias will withstand a lower temperature than Cinerarias, but neither will survive being frozen. If the winter proves to be a mild one, and you make provision for placing mats over the plants in frosty weather, you may succeed in keeping these plants through the winter in an unheated greenhouse.

All about Fuchsias

Q. Would you give a few practical notes on growing Fuchsias as I am anxious to take up their cultivation ?—*Sunbury.*

A. Fuchsias may be grown in pots for the greenhouse or window ; in window boxes either as tall plants or trained to hang down over the front of the boxes ; in baskets hanging from the greenhouse roof, in the flower garden, and in tubs. A half shaded position is one in which few flowering plants do well, yet for a window box with a northern aspect Fuchsias are the first plants I would recommend. Varying weather conditions in summer have comparatively little effect on Fuchsias. They are increased best by cuttings. Spring is the best time to put in cuttings. Vigorous young growths should be selected 2 to 3 inches in length. Remove the leaves from the lower half of the cutting close to the stem with a sharp knife, cutting the stem through immediately below the joint. One cutting may be placed in the centre of a small pot, or several round the side of one 4 inches in diameter. A suitable soil consists of equal parts of loam and leaf mould, with which should be mixed plenty of sand. Fuchsia cuttings will readily root under a bellglass or cloche in the window of a dwelling house, or, better still, in a warm greenhouse. The young plants will soon require potting, one being placed in a pot 1½ inches across. If grown for the greenhouse or window, or for planting outside during the summer months, the tip of the young shoot is removed when the plants are 4 to 6 inches high. To obtain tall pyramids the central shoot is supported by a strong stake, the side growths also being encouraged. The latter must be stopped as often as each shoot has made two pairs of leaves, till the plant attains the required size. For hanging baskets and window boxes I can strongly recommend Scarcity and Madame Cornellison. It will be found most convenient to use wire baskets, working the young plants at suitable distances between the wires. Remove the tips of the shoots when the young plants are 3 inches high. To prevent the soil falling between the wires line the baskets with moss. Standard Fuchsias are obtained by restricting each plant to one growth, removing all side shoots till the required height is reached. The top of the plant is then cut off and the points of the new shoots removed at intervals, to induce other growths to form a head. Good varieties are—Single : Madame Cornellison, white, red calyx ; Improved Rose of Castile, purple, white calyx; Scarcity, dark carmine red, light red calyx ; Amy Lye, salmon, white calyx ; Mrs. Rundle, salmon, flesh calyx ; Marirka, red self. Double : Ballet Girl, white, red calyx ; Phenomenal in three distinct colours, purple, rose, and white ; Pythagore, dark plum, red calyx ; and Madame Danjoux, white shaded mauve, carmine red calyx.

Ventilating Greenhouse

Q. Please give me a few hints on ventilating a greenhouse.—R. T., Windsor.

A. In spring the ventilation of glass houses is an important matter. The welfare of the plants depends entirely upon the attention of the owner. If an animal be shut up and then neglected it will soon die. Plants in greenhouses would, too, if the ventilators were kept closed during the greater part of each day, or on some

BEGONIA REX, A PLANT WITH HANDSOME FOLIAGE SUITABLE FOR THE SMALL GREENHOUSE.

THIS BEGONIA MAY BE INCREASED EASILY BY CUTTING THROUGH THE RIBS OF THE LEAF AND PLACING THIS ON SAND IN A WARM GREENHOUSE. LITTLE PLANTS WILL FORM AS SHOWN.

GLOXINIAS IN A GARDEN AT HAMPSTEAD, FROM SEED SOWN ON MAY 7TH, THE PLANTS WERE IN BLOOM IN OCTOBER.

days not opened at all. In winter time the plants would not suffer ; but in spring the young, tender shoots are growing and require plenty of fresh air. But the air must be admitted judiciously in order to prevent cold draughts blowing directly upon the foliage. The top ventilators of a greenhouse should, from March onwards, be opened slightly at 7 o'clock on fine mornings. Then increase the width a few inches at 9 o'clock, and again at 10 o'clock ; and if the outside air be warm and the sun shining brightly, open the front ventilators too at the last named hour. Commence reducing the amount of ventilation at 3 o'clock in the afternoon. The upper ventilators may be left open a little way each night during the summer. Usually both doors and ventilators may be opened wide in the middle of the day without detriment to the occupants of the house. The danger to avoid is keeping the house closed too long, until the interior becomes very hot, and then suddenly throwing open the ventilators and doors. The opening and closing is best done gradually.

Marguerite Leaves Ruined by Insect

Q. Will you tell me what causes those white streaks in Marguerites ? My Cinerarias were also similarly disfigured. I can find no insect.—*E. M. C., Bolton.*

A. The leaves received were badly attacked by the leaf mining maggot. Undoubtedly your Cinerarias are afflicted in the same way, for the Cineraria is subject to the attacks of the leaf miner. The larvae are living inside ; they tunnel their way between the tissues of the leaves. By holding the leaves to the light the position of the larvae may be readily seen. Since the culprits live within the leaves, it is exceedingly difficult to get rid of them. Although many remedies are sometimes recommended, the only certain cure is to remove the worst leaves and immediately burn them, and to kill the other grubs by pressing them between the finger and thumb. If this method is followed out from the first, and good growing conditions are also provided, injury from this pest will not be very great.

Geraniums for Winter Flowering

Q. Please tell me when I should take cuttings to raise a stock of Geraniums for winter flowering.—*E. J. K., Maldon.*

A. February is the time to insert cuttings to make strong plants for flowering in the winter in a warm greenhouse. The best cuttings are made from the tops of plants which have flowered in the greenhouse, but only strong and sturdy ones should be selected. They are best inserted singly in 2½- or 3-inch pots, according to their size. Plenty of sand and a little spent lime should be used in the compost, and the cuttings must be made quite firm in the soil. Water them in well, and then stand them on a light and airy shelf in the full sun. They will require but little water until rooted, but a dewing with the syringe twice a day will assist the emission of roots. Grow in cold frame in summer.

GOLDEN RAYED LILY (LILIUM AURATUM) GROWN IN, FLOWER POT.

Gloxinia Leaves and Buds for Examination

Q. For several years I have grown Gloxinias very successfully, but this year they are proving a failure. I enclose leaves and buds for your inspection, and shall be pleased if you can suggest the cause and a remedy, and how to prevent a recurrence next year.—*G. H. W., Chelmsford.*

A. The leaves and buds are seriously damaged by the rust mite (Tarsonymus tepidariorum), a very pernicious pest, as by its punctures of the leaves and tender parts of plants it not only abstracts their juices but causes the parts to become stunted, browned, and rusted, checking growth and spoiling the appearance of the plants. It is also a very difficult pest to suppress, particularly on Gloxinias and Gesneras, as from the woolliness of their leaves they are liable to be seriously affected by an insecticide. The whole mite family have a great dislike to sulphur, hence recourse is had to paraffin emulsion, 2 oz. to 1 gallon of water, adding ½ oz. of sulphide of potassium, and using as a spray. This, however, has a stunting effect on plants with hairy leaves, and I find it better to use tobacco water, or, better still, nicotine wash—1 oz. nicotine solution (98 per cent.) to 8¼ gallons of rain water, and spray the plants with this at intervals of three or four days about three times, and then at fortnightly or three weekly intervals to prevent recurrence of attack.

How to Get Rid of Woodlice

Q. My greenhouse is infested with woodlice. How can I get rid of them ?—*E. K., Wimborne.*

A. The most practical means of getting rid of them is trapping. If a little old hay or dry moss is placed in the bottom of a dirty flower pot with a little piece of cooked Potato, the woodlice will feed therein in great numbers. These traps should be emptied every morning, this will be found to have a wonderful effect in lessening the numbers of woodlice.

Green Fly in Conservatory

Q. I should be glad to know the best means of keeping down green fly which swarms on Roses and other plants in my conservatory.—*S. E., Mitcham.*

A. Undoubtedly the best means of keeping down green fly in a greenhouse is by fumigation. If you are not prepared to go to the expense of purchasing the concentrated preparations of nicotine for fumigating, the next best thing for you to do is to purchase tobacco rag from a horticultural sundriesman. All that is necessary is to drop a few handfuls of the tobacco rag on to two or three red hot pieces of coke from the furnace. Whilst smoking it must be carefully watched, flames must be kept down, otherwise it will be injurious to the plants near. Place the red hot coke in very small heaps on the path of the house about 15 feet apart, and remove the plants immediately over the fumes.

How to Grow Begonia Gloire de Lorraine

Q. I am anxious to grow this beautiful winter flowering Begonia. Will you please give me the essential details of cultivation ?—*Epping.*

A. With a greenhouse having four rows of hot water pipes, it should be a comparatively easy matter to keep the house at a sufficiently high temperature to suit the requirements of this highly decorative Begonia. A uniform night temperature of 50° F. is found to suit very well ; in the daytime the temperature will, of course, rise with the heat of the sun, when a little top air should be admitted. Yes ; it would be advisable to purchase plants now (September). In reference to the varieties which resemble Gloire de Lorraine, Turnford Hall and Caledonia are the best white forms, and Agatha has slightly larger flowers a little deeper in colour than the type. Plants purchased now would soon produce flowers, and these should all be picked off until the early spring, since this is the time when it is desired that they should be in full flower. Winter flowering Begonias in general need very careful watering, otherwise they will soon turn yellow and rot off at the base. The plants purchased at this season should be in their flowering pots, and would simply require careful attention to bring them into full blossom. These Begonias are increased by means of leaf cuttings taken in early spring. If a few of the older leaves are placed on a bed of sand in a propagating case in a hot house, young plants will form. When rooted these are potted up.

Taking Geranium Cuttings

Q. Is now (end of August) a suitable time to take Geranium cuttings for bedding out next summer ?—*A. H., Finchley.*

A. Cuttings for next season's stock should be procured as soon as possible. By careful examination of the plants, cuttings may be secured without spoiling the appearance of the flower beds. It is always worth the trouble to lay out the cuttings after being made on the floor of the potting shed for two days, but not to allow them to dry enough to cause the leaves to wither, only to flag slightly. Cuttings thus treated rarely, if ever, damp off when dibbled into boxes. Another precaution should, however, be taken to guard against this, and that is to stand the boxes of cuttings on trellises a few inches off the ground.

Fuchsias in Winter

Q. Last winter I lost a lot of my Fuchsias. Can you tell me how I can preserve them safely ?—*Anxious, Streatham.*

A. " I put my Fuchsias under the stages last winter, and when I came to take them out for repotting half of them were dead." This is a remark one often hears. They had not suffered from excess of moisture, but the reverse, for they were placed at the back of the water pipes, and became dried up. These most useful plants either for greenhouse or garden simply need to be kept from frost in winter ; a cool shed is an excellent place, but if they have to be located in the greenhouse they should be kept from the heat of pipes and the constant drip of the other plants on the stages above.

Plants for Greenhouse in Winter

Q. What are the best plants to put in my conservatory for the winter ? What in my window boxes ? What should be planted out in the garden now (October) ? Would Geranium and Carnation cuttings be likely to thrive in the conservatory (no fire) in the winter ? How can I fill up a draughty north-east bed ? What soil should be used for potting plants ?—*W. W. W., Worthing.*

A. You may have Azaleas, Arum Lilies, Deutzias, Spiraeas, Zonal Pelargoniums, Cinerarias, Primulas, Calceolarias, winter flowering Begonias, Cyclamens, and various kinds of bulbous plants in your conservatory for the winter months' display. In the window boxes and in the beds in the garden, bulbs such as Hyacinths, Tulips, Narcissi, Snowdrops, Scilla sibirica, Violas, Wallflowers, Myosotis, Silenes, Aubrietias, and Pansies. Wallflowers would be suitable for the draughty bed. If frost and excessive moisture can be excluded from the greenhouse Geraniums and Fuchsias would live in it through the winter. A good general potting compost consists of turfy soil, leaf soil, and sand.

Treatment of Various Orchids

Q. Will you give general instructions for treatment of Cypripedium, Odontoglossum, Dendrobium, and Cattleya ?—*E. A., Swindon.*

A. Cypripedium insigne, or Lady's Slipper, is one of the most easily cultivated of all Orchids. It succeeds in quite a cool house with such plants as Geraniums and Cinerarias, and may be stood in a cold frame in summer. It will stand several years in the same pans without changing the compost, and blossom finely each year. A minimum winter temperature of 40' to 45° will suit it, though a temperature 5° higher will not harm it. Well drained pots or pans are absolutely essential, and in each case from half to two-thirds of the pot should be filled with crooks. The compost should consist of 2 parts of good fibrous peat, 1 part of sphagnum, some coarse pieces of sandstone and charcoal, and clean crocks. If really good loam can be obtained a little may be used for C. insigne. All fine material should be sifted out and the rough pieces only used. Work the compost lightly about the roots, and be careful with watering until roots are active. Keep the water out of the growths at all times and fumigate frequently as a preventive of insects. Odontoglossum crispum and varieties must be grown in quite a cool house shaded from bright sun. By fire heat the house should never be allowed to rise above 40°. A compost similar to that recommended for the Cypripediums will do. The Dendrobiums require a high temperature, full sun, and an atmosphere heavily charged with moisture during the growing season. The temperature may rise above 100° with sun heat and ought not to drop below 70'. When growth is finished the water supply should be reduced and the plants placed in a cooler house with a drier atmosphere. A shelf exposed to full sun forms an ideal position. As the leaves die reduce the water supply until none at all is given. When the flower buds appear in spring place the plants in a warmer house again and give water sparingly until growth begins. They may be placed in hanging pots or baskets in a compost of fibrous peat, sphagnum, and charcoal. The Cattleya may be grown with the Cypripediums and a similar compost used. In all cases keep the floors and stages of the houses damp and the houses well ventilated.

Forcing Lily of the Valley

Q. I am anxious to have Lilies of the Valley in bloom in the greenhouse early in the year. Please advise.—*E. O. K., Leeds.*

A. September is the month in which to pot the roots intended for forcing. It is necessary to obtain plump, well matured crowns to commence with or failure will result; thus, if they have to be purchased it will be better to pay a little extra to a reliable nurseryman than to buy rubbish which cannot flower. In potting, use a somewhat light compost, consisting of turfy soil, leaf mould, and sand, placing six or eight crowns or single roots in a 5-inch pot. No good will result from cutting the roots about, unless, of course, they are too large for the pots, when they may be slightly trimmed. Let the tops of the crowns show just above the soil, and water them well in. Different growers have different ideas regarding the later treatment of the Lilies, but a very simple method is to plunge them in a box of cocoanut fibre over the hot water pipes in the greenhouse, well covering the crowns. It is important to keep the fibre in a moist condition, when growth will soon commence. They can be removed when growing strongly and gradually introduced to the full daylight to bring them to their proper colour.

Marguerites Suddenly Withering

Q. I am sending you two Marguerites which have suddenly withered and died. I should like to know the reason why, as I have lost a good few in this way. Other Marguerites in the same beds and window boxes are looking very healthy. Last year I lost some in the same way, plants very much larger than those I am sending you, in fact, one measured over 1 yard in diameter. I should esteem it a favour if you can tell the cause and how to remedy it, as I am afraid my beds will soon begin to look unsightly. —*Marguerite, Sussex.*

A. The plants are infested by the Sclerotium disease, a parasitic fungus which probably attacks and kills more plants of different species, and belonging to widely separated orders, than any other. The disease first shows itself in the sudden cessation of growth in the plants. Upon examination the roots and rootstem are found to be dead, and on them, usually at or near the ground line, appears a very delicate white mould encircling the stem. The mycelium also penetrates into the interior, and gradually extends upwards. Finally the stem becomes dry and brittle and falls down. The whitish fluffy mould first seen soon changes to a brownish colour, and liberates clouds of minute spores when rubbed. This is the earliest and most frequent form under which the fungus appears, and is called the Botrytis or summer stage. In Potatoes, Beans, and other plants with hollow stems, the mycelium or spawn grows up inside the stem, and there forms numerous irregularly shaped solid bodies varying in shape from that of a Mustard seed to that of a grain of wheat. In the Chrysanthemum and other plants of a semi-ligneous nature, these bodies are formed just beneath the bark, and somewhat more sparsely and much smaller. They are at first white or pale in colour, but become black outside when mature, and are called sclerotia, and give name to the fungus, viz. Sclerotinia sclerotiorum. They remain in this condition until the following season, when, owing to the decay of the host plant previously, and thus liberated, they produce spores which infest a new crop. The prevalence of the sclerotium disease is due to plants containing sclerotia being left on the land, or in the dead plants being thrown on the rubbish heap, and their remains as vegetable mould being returned to the land. It is important, therefore, to remove and burn all plants infested by the disease. Gas lime or quick lime should be applied to the land.

Making and Planting a Window Box

Q. I should be glad of a few hints on the above subject.—*Suburban.*

A. The box should be made about 2 inches wider than the window sill, and 7 inches deep. Bore a number of holes through the bottom of the box to drain away all surplus water, and paint the outside of the box dark green. Use ¾-inch boards. Wedges may be used to make the box stand level on the window sills. Put in cinders 2 inches deep for drainage, and use a compost of loam and leaf soil in equal proportions. Scarlet Geraniums, white Marguerites, and blue Lobelia ; or Fuchsias, single flowered Petunias, and Lobelia would make good combinations. Put in the plants in May. Carnations are admirable plants for a window box ; they should be allowed to droop over the edge.

Selection of Plants for Window Box

Q. Will you please give a list of plants suitable for growing in a window box ?—*E. A. T., Sutton.*

A. The following list of plants that may be grown in windows will be useful for reference : Bulbs of different sorts, especially Crocuses, Snowdrops, and Hyacinths ; Cactus, various kinds ; Arum Lily, Richardia aethiopica ; Campanula pyramidalis ; Creeping Jenny ; Echeveria ; Euonymus variegatus ; Indiarubber Plant, Ficus elastica ; Fuchsias, various kinds ; Geraniums, various ; Hydrangea ; orange coloured Lily, Imantophyllum ; Ivy-leaved Geranium ; Ivies, various kinds ; lemon scented Verbena ; golden rayed Lily, L. auratum ; Lobelias, various kinds ; Lily of the Valley ; Mother of Thousands, Saxifraga ; Musk ; Myrtle ; Oak-leaf Geranium ; Orange Tree ; Saxifrages, various sorts ; Vallota purpurea, Scarboro' Lily.

Window Box Plants for Winter

Q. What can I put in my window boxes for the winter now that the Geraniums and other flowers are over ?—*Anxious, Bury.*

A. Window boxes are too frequently stored out of sight at this season ; but they may be utilised for the reception of several different kinds of shrub. Variegated Euonymus, Cupressus, Hollies, Box, and others, can all be purchased in small pots at no great price ; these, if plunged in the soil of the boxes, with a few bulbs intermingled, will provide a cheerful if not brilliant display, which will be found far preferable to the blanks caused by the removal of the boxes. Small plants of variegated Ivy can be secured for draping the front of the boxes.

Treatment of Newly Potted Bulbs

Q. I am told that newly potted bulbs should be plunged for five or six weeks so as to encourage the formation of roots before top growth starts. Could I use sawdust for covering them ?—*E. A. T., Rugby.*

A. Yes ; you may plunge the pots containing the bulbs in sawdust, but ordinary sand would be far more suitable—it is better than ashes. Crocuses, Snowdrops, Tulips, Hyacinths and Narcissi should all be plunged in the same way.

Rose of Jericho

Q. I should be glad of a few particulars of this extraordinary plant.—*Amateur, S. Wales.*

A. This is a common name for Anastatica Hierochuntina, which is also known as one of the Resurrection Plants. This plant recovers its original form, however dry it may be, on immersion in water, but it is not true that it will come into full flower in so short a space of time. This curious plant is in fact an annual, the leaves of which fall off after flowering; the branches and branchlets then become dry, hard, and ligneous, curling inwards at their extremities. Even after the lapse of many years in this dry state the plant will resume its vitality on being placed in water. It is a native of Syria and the Mediterranean region, and when in a dry round ball it is readily blown about the sea shore. By some commentators it is supposed to be the "rolling thing before the whirlwind" mentioned by Isaiah.

About Tuberoses

Q. When is the best time to pot up Tuberoses to provide blossom in the greenhouse in summer ?—*E. K. J., Sussex.*

A. April is a suitable time to pot the bulbs of Tuberoses to flower during the summer. Suitable pots are those of the 3½- or 4-inch sizes. The Tuberoses like turfy soil, and leaf mould, decayed manure, and sand should be included. It will be necessary to plunge them in cocoanut fibre, and if this is directly over the hot water pipes so much the better. One watering immediately after potting is all that is required till growth commences, although if close to the pipes the fibre should be kept moist. When growing freely remove to 6-inch pots, place on a sunny shelf, and water more liberally, giving occasional applications of liquid manure.

CHAPTER VI

All about Chrysanthemums

Taking Chrysanthemum Cuttings

Q. Will you tell me when and how to take Chrysanthemum cuttings ?—*E. H., Staines.*

A. When the plants have finished flowering let them get a little dry at the roots, then cut them down to within 6 inches of the soil. They should be exposed to the open air for a day or two, as this will make the cuttings firm and not so likely to fail. They are best struck in 3-inch pots, which should be perfectly clean and well crocked to ensure thorough drainage. Fill up the pots nearly to the rims with soil, and press it down firmly, and over this place a sprinkling of silver sand. The strongest cuttings should be selected and taken off with a sharp knife ; they should be about 3 or 4 inches long. Cut off a few of the lower leaves, and they will then be ready for inserting in the pots. Four or five cuttings should be inserted round the sides of the pots, and the soil should be pressed firmly about them. This done, sprinkle them with water. If the cuttings are wintered in a frame the pots should be placed on a layer of ashes. Keep the frame shut up close till the cuttings have taken root, then admit air on every favourable occasion to prevent them from becoming drawn. During frosty weather the frame should be covered over with mats. Those who have a greenhouse can winter their cuttings with more ease and safety, and nothing suits them better than to be placed on a shelf near the glass.

Chrysanthemums for blooming in November and December

Q. Please give me a list of varieties that will bloom at this season. I shall grow them in the border, and pot up in September and bring into the greenhouse.—*I. O. H., Wanstead.*

A. The following are suitable varieties, namely, Source d'Or ; White and Yellow Selborne ; Kathleen Thompson, A. J. Balfour, Mrs. W. Knox, Crimson Source d'Or, Dr. Enguehard, Madame R. Oberthur, Princess Victoria, white, also yellow Princess Victoria,

OUTDOOR CHRYSANTHEMUM MAGGIE (LIGHT YELLOW).

W. H. Lincoln, Tuxedo, La Triomphante, Winter Cheer, Souvenir d'une Petite Amie, Jason, Mr. F. S. Vallis, J. H. Silsbury, Mrs. G. Beach, L. Canning. Mrs. J. C. Neville, Roi des Blancs, Western King, and Christmas Crimson.

On "Stopping" Certain Chrysanthemums

Q. Will you give directions as to stopping the shoots of the following varieties?—*O. T. E., Chester.*

A. Assuming that you wish to grow the plants for the production of blooms for the early November shows, you should treat the plants as follows. Henry Perkins and Madame Carnot, stop March 20th, and take second crown buds. Chrysanthemum Leroux, Joseph Rocher, Mr. F. S. Vallis, Countess of Warwick, Capt. P. Scott, and George Lock should be allowed to make natural breaks, and first crowns be taken in August. Miss Lily Mountford, J. H. Silsbury and Vicar of Leatherhead, stop April 20th, second crowns. Madame R. Oberthur, Emily Mileham, and Bessie Godfrey, stop May 20th, first crowns. Miss Mildred Ware, Lady Randolph, and N.C.S. Jubilee, stop April 10th, second crowns. Ben Wells, stop March 20th, second crowns. Mrs. F. Judson, stop May 5th, first crowns. Merstham Yellow is an early flowering variety, and should only be stopped once, at the end of April. Western King is a late flowering variety, and should be stopped twice, in April and in June.

How to Grow Chrysanthemums

Q. I have (November) bought three dozen Chrysanthemums in bloom; they are in 8-inch pots. I have had them about five weeks. Some of them are over now, but there is new growth starting. I bought these with the object of increasing them next year. Now some of my friends say bury the pots as they are in the open, some say stand them in a cold frame, and all say you will get some shoots for cuttings next spring. I would like your advice.—*H. W., Clissold Park.*

A. When all the flowers have faded place the pots in a cold frame, or, failing a frame, in a greenhouse close to the glass, to prevent the young shoots being drawn up weakly. Cut off the old stems 6 inches above the soil level ; they are now useless. In March next you may use the young sucker shoots—those growing through the soil—for increasing the stock ; they will root readily enough in sandy soil when inserted as cuttings. The cuttings will grow into fine flowering plants next autumn.

H

OUTDOOR CHRYSANTHEMUM WHITE ST. CROUTTS.

How to Cure Chrysanthemum Rust

Q. My plants are badly affected with this reddish fungus. What can I do to cure it or prevent its appearance another year ?— *Anxious, Surbiton.*

A. Take the cuttings in December, sooner or later as convenient, trim the leaves off the cuttings, and do not leave more foliage than is absolutely necessary ; do not cut the bases off, label each lot of cuttings, and bury them in sulphur in a close fitting box—a biscuit box would do. Use plenty of sulphur so as to cover the cuttings.

CHRYSANTHEMUM CUTTINGS.   BAD ON LEFT ; GOOD
ON RIGHT.

Leave them in the box for twenty-four hours, then take out, cut off the bases and insert in the usual way. The cuttings will flag a little, but will soon pick up after being put in the cutting box. If possible strike them in another house, apart from the house in which they flowered, or even in a cold frame. This treatment invariably effects a cure : you may follow it with confidence.

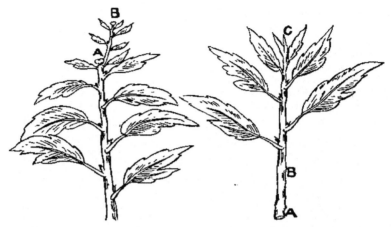

UNSUITABLE CUTTING, CONTAINS
FLOWER BUD AT A. BUDS
WILL FORM PREMATURELY
AS AT B.

SUITABLE CUTTING PREPARED
FOR INSERTION. LEAF RE-
MOVED AT A, B, STEM CUT
THROUGH AT A.

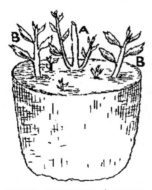

STEM CUTTINGS (UNSUIT-
ABLE) ARE SHOWN AT A.
GOOD CUTTINGS (FROM
SOIL) ARE SHOWN AT B.

A SHOWS BLUNT STICK FOR MAKING
HOLE FOR CUTTING. NOTE THAT
SAND FALLS IN HOLE FROM SUR-
FACE FOR BASE OF CUTTING (B)
TO REST ON.

Chrysanthemums Unsatisfactory

Q. Herewith I send you leaves of Chrysanthemums. I shall be grateful if you will tell me the cause of the trouble and the cure.— *W. G. A., Arundel.*

A. The leaves of the Chrysanthemums are infested with a leaf-mining grub. Gather the bad leaves and burn them. Your plants need stimulants. Feed them with clear soot water, liquid manure and

"TAKING" CHRYSANTHEMUM BUDS.

TERMINAL BUD SECURED BY REMOVING OTHERS.

CROWN BUD SHOWN AT A : THIS WOULD NOT DEVELOP UNLESS SHOOTS B WERE REMOVED WHEN SMALL.

artificials judiciously. The Carnations are also suffering from rust. Pick off the leaves affected, and carefully syringe the plants with the Bordeaux mixture. Use copper sulphate 1 lb., soda crystals 1½ lb., water 11½ gallons ; or you may use verdigris 1 lb., water 12 gallons. Spray the plants thoroughly.

Treatment of Chrysanthemums

Q. What artificial manure do you recommend for Chrysanthemums after they are housed ? For the last three or four years I have grown some fine plants of Chrysanthemum, which have produced very promising buds. I try to grow them on to what I think is the best bud for each individual variety, the buds appearing ready for taking generally from the first week of August until the middle of September. When housed, as a rule, my plants are perfectly clean and healthy, but the buds do not develop as I anticipate, considering the health and strength of the plants. I fancy it is something to do with feeding after they are housed. I have so far restricted myself to pure Peruvian guano, keeping the house and atmosphere as dry as I can with a temperature of 50˙ to 55˙. Would you also tell me what you think is the best bud to take to get good blooms of Mrs. A. T. Miller, Rose Pockett, Pockett's Surprise, Formality, and Splendour ?—*Chrysanthemum, Upper Norwood.*

A. It is quite possible that you have taken first crown buds too early, and that the petals have not, in consequence, opened as freely, and developed into as large flowers as they would if buds were taken ten days or a fortnight later. Furthermore, you may have crippled the roots by over feeding. Clay's Fertilizer, guano and other concentrated manures are suitable for feeding the plants after the latter are placed under glass. The best buds to take of the following varieties, Formality, Mrs. A. T. Miller, Rose Pockett, Pockett's Surprise, and Splendour, are second crown buds.

Outdoor Chrysanthemums in Winter

Q. Will you tell me how to preserve outdoor Chrysanthemums during the winter ? The situation is rather low. Last winter after I had cut them down I covered them well over with ashes, but lost every one.—*B. J. C., Melton Mowbray.*

A. If you have a cold frame, the best way is to take them up and plant them thickly together in the frame, covering with mats in very severe weather, planting in the borders again towards the end of March. If you have not a frame, we should take them up and plant at the foot of a south warm wall, packing some dry leaves well round them, but not covering up the top of the plants. On very severe nights cover over with mats or litter. In this way you should have no difficulty in preserving your plants through the winter.

CHAPTER VII

Failures with Bulbous Flowers—How to Avoid Them

Gladioli not Flowering

Q. I planted a lot of Gladiolus bulbs in March, very few of which flowered the same year. Are they likely to be of any use another year?—*H. C., Southsea.*

A. If you lift, dry, and store the bulbs until the early part of spring, they will probably flower next year. They have not been strong enough to do so this year. The bulbs must be of sufficient size, and be well ripened to produced flower spikes.

Daffodils, Tulips, etc., for Exhibition

Q. Please inform me the best varieties of Daffodils, Tulips, and any other kind of bulbs suitable for exhibition. Also the best time to pot same for exhibiting the early part of April, and whether to keep pots in cold greenhouse or outside.—*Carnation, Gosport.*

A. Daffodils : Emperor, M. J. Berkeley, Mrs. Walter Ware, J. B. M. Camm, Madame de Graaff, Gloria Mundi, Sir Watkin, Barrii conspicuus, Albatross, Duchess of Westminster, John Bain, Poeticus ornatus. The above varieties represent the chief sections into which Daffodils are divided. A representative section such as this should find favour with the judges, in preference to all yellow trumpet or bicolor varieties, for instance. The sorts named can all be obtained at a reasonable price. Early single Tulips : White, Joost van Vondel, King of the Yellows, Rose Gris de Lin, Prince of Austria, Couleur Cardinal, and Duchesse de Parme. May flowering single Tulips : Clara Butt, Bouton d'Or, Pride of Haarlem, Mrs. Farncombe Sanders, La Tulipe Noire, Picotee. Hyacinths would be excellent bulbs for you to grow for exhibition ; good varieties are Vuurbaak, crimson ; Cavaignac, pale rose pink ; Mont Blanc, white ; Grandeur à Merveille, pale blush ; Captain Boyton, lilac blue ; General Havelock, dark blue ; Bird of Paradise, yellow. Pot up the bulbs in October, plunge them in ashes for about six weeks, then, if rooting freely, remove to a cold frame till February, plunging the pots to the rims in ashes. Towards the end of February place them in a cold greenhouse. If too early you can retard them by shading from the sun, and keeping abundance of air on the house. If you decide to grow the May flowering Tulips, bring these into your greenhouse a month earlier.

Bulbs from Stem of Tiger Lily

Q. Will you tell me whether the enclosed bulbs (taken from joints of stem of Tiger Lily) will bloom the first year, and also any special preparation as regards soil and growth ?—J. Hewlett, Bow.

FOUR TULIP BULBS POTTED IN 5-INCH WIDE POT.

A. The bulbs you speak of, which have been taken from the stems of Tiger Lilies, will not flower next year, or for two or three years to come, most likely. You may get flowers the third year after the bulbils have been formed, or an odd one or two may even appear the second year, but this is very unlikely. The best way to grow them is to make up a bed of peat and sandy loam in about equal proportions, about 6 inches deep, on well drained ground. Plant the bulbils from 1 inch to 2 inches below the surface, on a bed of silver sand, and scatter a little more sand on them before covering them with soil. In two years' time lift, sort into large and small, and replant.

FIVE DAFFODIL BULBS IN 6-INCH POT. SOIL HAS STILL TO BE ADDED, AND WILL HALF COVER THE BULBS.

THREE HYACINTH BULBS IN A 6-INCH FLOWER POT. THESE AND TULIP BULBS SHOULD BE HALF COVERED WITH SOIL.

Lilies Diseased

Q. Will you please tell me the probable cause of enclosed Liliums dying off? Both blooms and leaves are falling. I cannot account for it, unless it is because I have given them on two occasions weak manure water (sheep's). I have nearly a dozen varieties of Liliums, in my garden. I should like to give the ground a good digging this autumn or winter. Shall I leave the bulbs in and not disturb them or take them out and put in again, as I have done each previous year? — F. B., Bow.

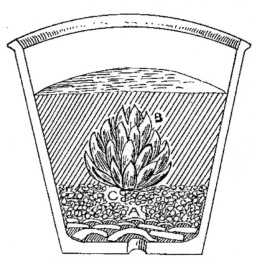

HOW A LILY BULB IS POTTED.

A. Your Lilies are affected with one of the diseases that of late years have attacked these lovely subjects. There is little you can do to stay its progress. Some Lily growers, when their bulbs have been attacked, have taken them up and placed them in bags of sulphur, allowing this substance to percolate well among the scales. Replanted the next year they have shown no signs of the disease. We should certainly advise you to take up the bulbs and replant again after turning over the ground as you propose. In replanting place a little peat beneath each bulb and surround it with ½ inch of sand. L. auratum should be planted 8 inches deep, and L. umbellatum about 5 inches.

About Lily Bulbs

Q. I have three Lilies (Lilium auratum) which have just finished flowering—two of the pots contained seventeen and thirteen blooms respectively—and now I do not know how to treat them. Should

ONE OF THE FINEST OF ALL DAFFODILS FOR THE GARDEN,
SIR WATKIN, PALE YELLOW.

they be put outside and repotted in the spring?—*A. K. C., North umberland.*

A. Place the pots containing the bulbs in a cool frame and gradually withhold water.   In spring repot them in small pots so that you can transfer them to larger ones in due course.

Growing Lilies in Pots

Q. I am anxious to grow Lilies in pots.   Which are the best for the purpose? and how are they grown?—*H. E. W., Ramsgate.*

CROCUS SIR WALTER SCOTT, GROWN IN FLOWER POT IN COLD GREENHOUSE.

A. The potting should be done at any time during the resting season of the bulbs, preferably in autumn. A good soil is made by mixing together loam and peat in equal parts, and adding smaller quantities of sharp silver sand and charcoal broken to the size of Hazel Nuts. Deep potting should be practised so as to leave space above the bulbs for top dressing later on when growth is being made.   Speciosum varieties, auratum and candidum are the most useful.

Gladiolus Bulbs

Q. Last season I grew a lot of Gladioli The Bride, and some hybrids in pots in heated greenhouse.   Would these bulbs be worth growing in pots another year?—*Rosa, Derby.*

A. You can grow these on another year and they would succeed very well.   The bulbs should be shaken free of soil and hung up in an airy shed, until the sap has gone out of their foliage, when they may be cleaned and placed in dry sand or bags, and kept in a cool, dry place ready for another season.

Room Plants

Room Plants Failing

Q. Will you please tell me what is wrong with my Aspidistra— why the leaves that have grown up tall all split, and why all the new leaves that come up now have taken to be so short? They unfold so quickly and do not grow at all.—*E. B., Kensington.*

A. The leaves have most likely been knocked by people passing by, especially when they were young and tender. As the young leaves lack vigour the plant evidently needs dividing and repotting. If unable to do this take it to the florist. Turfy soil 2 parts, sand and leaf soil 1 part, make up a good soil mixture. February or early March is a good time to repot. This plant, when well rooted, needs a lot of water in summer and comparatively little in winter.

Norfolk Island Pine (Araucaria excelsa) in Room

Q. I have a fine plant of this in my dining room. It is full grown, six tiers high, the lower branches still on and quite healthy, but the roots show on the top of the pot, also at the bottom, and I am told they object to repotting. I do not want to lose it by so doing; can you please advise me as to how it should be dealt with? —*M. M. C. W., Essex.*

A. If the pot is well filled with roots it will be advisable to repot the plant in spring. Use a mixture of fibrous loam and peat in equal proportions, and sand to make the whole porous. Press down the new soil carefully and firmly, and see that the soil never gets too dry or is kept in a saturated condition, and then the tree will improve in every way.

Repotting Room Plants

Q. Can you give me a few hints on repotting room plants?— *S. T. E., Ealing.*

A. Room plants should be examined in February, and if roots in large numbers have reached the side of the pot, repotting is necessary. I refer to such subjects as Aspidistras, palms, and various ferns which are used for indoor decoration. Unless the plant is to be returned to a pot of the same size as was previously occupied it will not be advisable to disturb the roots a great deal. For some time after potting watering must be carefully performed, giving it only when the soil is fairly dry, or sourness of the soil will result.

CHAPTER VIII

Grape Growing in Greenhouses

Vine for Unheated Greenhouse

Q. I have an unheated greenhouse. Can I grow Grapes there with any measure of success?—*E. S. T., Finchley.*

A. Quite easily. Excellent crops may be had from an unheated greenhouse provided (1) this is in a sunny place, (2) the proper varieties are grown, (3) that certain simple cultural details are attended to. The first thing is to make a good border. Dig out a hole 3 feet across and 3 feet deep. Put a layer of bricks in the bottom for drainage and a layer of turves, grass side downwards, on these. Then fill the hole with turfy soil (turves each chopped into about 6 pieces with a spade) with which a good sprinkling of half inch bones and one fourth part well rotted manure were previously mixed. Do not plant within a fortnight; this will allow the soil to settle down. A properly prepared border is of the first importance.

Q. Does it matter whether the Vine is planted out of doors or inside the vinery?

A. It makes no real difference providing the border is well made. The Vine is hardy, frost will not harm it. If planted outside, however, it is wise to protect that part of the stem that is out of doors by wrapping it round well with straw or hay.

Q. Which are the most suitable varieties?

A. Black Hamburgh is the best of the black Grapes for this purpose; Foster's Seedling, Buckland Sweetwater and Royal Muscadine are suitable white sorts.

Q. When should vines be planted?

A. In March just as growth is about to commence, or in autumn or winter.

Pruning Vines

Q. How are Vines pruned?—*Ignorant, Windsor.*

A. Newly planted Vines are cut down to within a foot of the base. One shoot is allowed to grow to form the future stem or rod;

BLACK HAMBURGH GRAPE IN AMATEUR'S GREENHOUSE IN LONDON SUBURB.

all the others are rubbed off. If there is room for two stems then two may be allowed to develop. The following year the Vine may be left 3 feet long ; each year 3 feet of new stem is left until the allotted space is filled. Meantime side growths will form. Some of the best, at intervals of 15 to 18 inches apart, are allowed to grow ; others are rubbed off in spring when quite small. Those shoots left are called laterals and will form spurs.

Pruning Lateral Shoots.

Q. How are lateral shoots or spurs pruned ?—*Ignorant, Windsor.*

A. The pruning is simplicity itself. Each year (in January) the previous summer's growth is cut back to within two buds of the base, thus practically all the previous year's growth is cut away. When these two buds start into growth in spring only one is retained ; if neither contains a bunch then the weaker is rubbed off ; if one

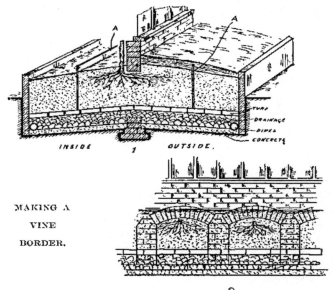

MAKING A
VINE
BORDER.

contains a bunch and the other does not, naturally the former is retained. The embryo bunch can be distinguished when the shoot is only an inch long.

Treatment of Vines during Summer

Q. Would you give general directions for treatment of Vines during the summer months ?—*Ignorant, Windsor.*

A. The side shoots are "stopped" at one leaf beyond the bunch ; if the shoot bears no bunch then it is stopped when it has made five leaves. Further shoots that grow are stopped beyond one leaf. Until the top of the vinery is reached the leading shoot is allowed to grow unchecked, 3 feet only of the summer's growth being left at the January pruning. A moist, warm atmosphere is necessary until the Grapes begin to colour, then more air and less moisture are essential. Avoid giving much air at once ; the ventilators should be opened gradually. Allow the

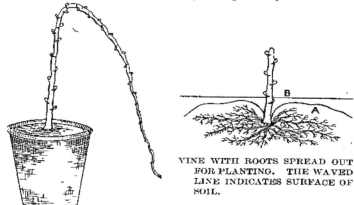

VINE WITH ROOTS SPREAD OUT FOR PLANTING. THE WAVED LINE INDICATES SURFACE OF SOIL.

VINE AS RECEIVED FROM THE NURSERY.

temperature to rise 10° above the minimum night temperature before air is given. When the Vines are in bloom more air and less moisture than usual should be the order of the day. When the Grapes are about the size of Black Currants they apparently cease to make any progress for two or three weeks ; this is the "stoning" period, the period of seed formation. Thinning the berries when they are about the size of Peas is an important item of work. When the Grapes are cut the Vines need full exposure. They cannot then have too much air. If cut with about 4 inches of growth, Grapes will keep for weeks in a cool, airy, dark or shaded room. The piece of

I

growth is inserted in a bottle of water, the bottles being fixed on a shelf, slantingly, so that the bunch may hang free.

Vines not Fruiting

Q. I have five Vines (they are twenty-five years old) in a leanto greenhouse facing south-east. They are trained on wires; the border is outside, made and drained. I cut down the old canes to about 3 feet from the border because they did not produce fruit, and trained up young canes in their places. The young canes are

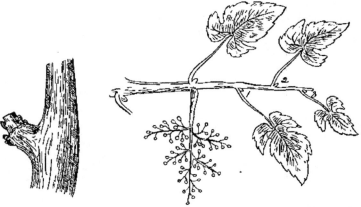

SIDE SHOOT OR LATERAL OF VINE AS PRUNED IN JANUARY.   ONE OF THE BUDS WILL GIVE RISE TO A SHOOT LIKE THIS WHICH IN SUMMER IS STOPPED TWO OR THREE JOINTS BEYOND THE BUNCH.

healthy and have plenty of foliage, but where the fruit ought to be they produce tendrils.—*J. W., Essex.*

A. The reason the young rods have not borne bunches is, no doubt, owing to lack of maturity. If the house is heated, keep the pipes warm during the autumn and admit plenty of air in the day-time and even at night, to ripen the wood. In December, just before Christmas, prune back the young rods to within 3 feet or so of the base of the current year's growth; do this each year until the allotted space is covered. Also top dress the borders with good fibrous loam and some bone meal. It is probable that the variety you have needs a warmer temperature than you give it. Muscat of

Alexandria, Madresfield Court, Cannon Hall Muscat, Muscat Hamburgh and Mrs. Pince are useless in an unheated house.

Grapes Spoilt

Q. Will you tell me how to prevent Lady Downe's Grapes from going bad as per berries enclosed? The Vine is very old, and is grown in the same house as Black Hamburgh. I have the roof shaded over

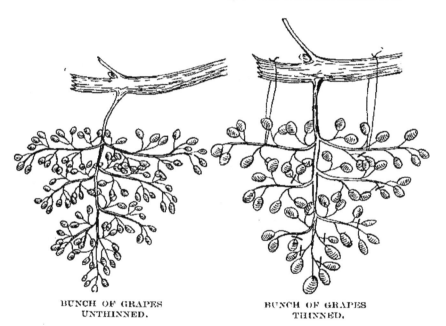

BUNCH OF GRAPES
UNTHINNED.

BUNCH OF GRAPES
THINNED.

the Lady Downe's, and ventilators open about 6.30 a.m. I have the same trouble more or less every year about stoning time and although I did not thin them so hard I have had to cut away a lot of berries, which has spoilt the look of the bunches. The house is not heated regularly, only on dreary, cold, and wet nights.— *W. Foster, Acton.*

A. Your Grapes are badly scalded. The variety Lady Downe's is more liable to scalding than any other, since it has such a thin skin.

Scalding is always worse when a bright spell of weather comes after a prolonged dull one, especially if at the time when the berries are stoning, *i.e.* when the stones are hardening, and before colouring commences. In addition to the free ventilation and light shading given, admit a little air all night and warm the pipes too ; this is all you can do. When the top ventilators are left open an inch or two all night, the berries are rarely scalded. Scalding is caused by the sun shining on the Grapes when they are moist. If the ventilator is left open the moisture does not settle on the Grapes.

Foster's Seedling Grape Spotted

Q. Can you tell me the reason of my white Grapes being spotted in this way ? I enclose a bunch.—*E. W., Hendon.*

A. The spots on the berries of your Grapes are the result of the atmosphere of the vinery being kept too cold and too damp. When Grapes are quite ripe it is the inevitable result that decay follows unless the air of the house is kept sufficiently warm and dry to prevent it.

Grapes Shrivelling before Ripe

Q. I am much disappointed in my Grapes. The berries and the stalks shrivel, rendering the fruit quite useless.—*H. E. S., Oxon.*

A. The shrivelling of the berries is due to shanking, a failing brought about by a number of causes, the chief being a sour and badly drained border. At the same time the berries will shank if the border is allowed to become dry, and it should be borne in mind that Vines from the time of starting until the time of colouring need copious supplies of water, with occasional applications of liquid manure. Examine the border frequently, and never allow it to become dry. The fumes from burning sulphur are, as you have learnt, very injurious to growing Vines, but we attribute the shanking either to sour soil or to overcropping the previous year.

Top Dressing Vine Borders

Q. What is the best material with which to top dress Vine borders ? Can I use fowl manure ?—*A. E. W., Walsall.*

A. Cow manure is by far the best, but as you are unable to procure it the fowl manure may be used as a substitute. It should first of all be mixed with about its own bulk of turfy soil, and then spread over the borders to a depth of 2 or 3 inches. Horse litter may also be given, but not in the fresh state. When half rotted it may be spread evenly over the border.

About a Greenhouse and Neglected Vines

Q. I write to ask your advice about a greenhouse I have. It is 50 by 14 feet, and contains no stage or shelves. It is 3 feet high at sides, and 9 feet high at the apex. Can I grow vegetables in it? or what would be more profitable? I have a Vine that has not been pruned for three years. Can I cut it hard back?—*Constant Reader, Stockport.*

A. You may force Rhubarb and Seakale in the greenhouse in the winter months, and grow Mushrooms, early Lettuces, and, later Kidney Beans, in pots or boxes. In summer time you cannot do better than grow Tomatoes. The proper time to prune the Vine is at the end of December, but if you cut away the growths of several years hard back to the main rod, side shoots will grow again, but there would be little fruit the same year. The best plan would be to prune to the base of the shoots of this year's growth, leaving two buds only. There would be long spurs, but it is not possible to avoid them unless you cut hard back, and sacrifice most of the fruit for a year or two. This would be best in the end; it would give the Vines a new lease of life and result in fresh vigorous growths.

Treatment of Ripening Grapes

Q. My Grapes are just beginning to colour. Should I still continue syringing and damping down the path and walls? and if so, how long? They are mostly Black Hamburgh and Alicante.—*C. N., Hampstead.*

A. You must cease syringing the Vines, but damping down should continue a little longer, say for two or three weeks, although it must be gradually diminished. On dull, wet days it will not be necessary at all.

Grapes Failing

Q. I am sending a bunch of Black Alicante, and should feel very grateful if you could tell me the reason of their disfigurement. I have two Vines, and for two or three years have had occasional bunches go in the same way, but this year every bunch is affected; I have about twenty bunches on each Vine. The Vine itself seems quite healthy. I have the border inside, so that I keep it in good condition. I do not force them at all—just have a little heat when they begin to grow, generally about March, until warm weather sets in. Is it lack of heat? Gros Colmar and a white Muscat do well in same house. I shall have had them nine or ten years.—*A Lady Gardener, Suffolk.*

A. Your Vines are affected with what is known as scald. It is caused through inefficient ventilation, especially on bright, sunny mornings whilst the vinery and even the berries are damp with condensed moisture. It usually attacks Grapes when they have nearly finished stoning. There is no cure for the berries once affected. The way to prevent its attack is to ventilate freely as soon as the berries have commenced to stone, until they have done stoning and are commencing to colour. The ventilators, both front and top, should be thrown wide open in front of the Vines in warm weather during the day, and a little air must be left on all night.

Treatment of Vine

Q. Will you please give me information as to the treatment of a Black Hamburgh Vine? I have gathered all the Grapes and the leaves are fast dying off, and I am now at a loss what to do. The previous owner of the Vine advised me to lift it down from the glass and lay it on the floor of the greenhouse to rest, also to place a small load of cow manure on the roots in January. Is this the correct treatment? I know that the laterals should be pruned back to two buds ; but when?—*W. S. S., Notts.*

A. The Vine needs little or no attention now. Its chief need is fresh air, so that the growth may ripen well ; therefore keep the house cold by opening the ventilators wide. Pruning may be done in December or January. Each of the side shoots is cut back to the two lowest buds on the past summer's growth. A dressing of cow manure on the outside border in January would be advisable ; strawy litter would be better, putting on and forking in the cow manure in March. The strawy litter would be warmer as a winter covering.

Sulphuring Hot Water Pipes in a Vinery for the Destruction of Red Spider

Q. Would you kindly advise me if it would be safe to use sulphur and lime on the hot water pipes in a vinery in which the Grapes are ripe and in which there is a lot of Maidenhair Ferns and other plants? I have no other house for plants, and later on there will be all the bedding plants and Chrysanthemums. Kindly advise me as to the best time to clean the house.—*No.* 53, *Bucks*.

A. It is quite safe to sulphur the hot water pipes in a vinery in which the Grapes are ripe, provided it is not done excessively, otherwise there is danger of injuriously affecting the skin of white Grapes such as Muscat of Alexandria, White Frontignan, and indeed all white varieties, the fumes turning the skin to a bluish colour, and to some extent detracting from their appearance. But as you say there are a number of Maidenhair Ferns and other plants in the house, it would not be safe to use the sulphur on the hot water pipes, as the fumes will certainly injure the more tender of the growths and cause them to become brown. The better plan would be to use a sponge and go over the leaves carefully, the sponge being moistened with a soft soap solution, 2 oz. or 3 oz. soft soap to 1 gallon of water, and thus break up the webs and remove most of the pests by the process. This is a tedious but a sure way of palliating the evil, and would be the best.

Rust on Muscat Grapes

Q. Enclosed is a sample of Muscat of Alexandria Grape, being the first fruit of a four year old Vine with an outside border. The Vines were started in the first week of February. The brown marks on the Grapes were noticed about a fortnight ago (August).— *Enquirer, Newbury*.

A. The Muscat of Alexandria Grapes are affected by rust. Overheating of the pipes while the berries were small would cause the mischief. If the roots of the Vines are in a cold border, this condition of affairs would be aggravated ; violent changes in the temperature are also likely to predispose the Vines to this malady.

Vine Leaves Diseased

Q. Can you tell me what is the matter with the Vine leaves enclosed ? They seem in a bad way. What can I do to cure them ?— *A. E. T., Bury*.

A. Your Vines are suffering from a bad attack of thrips, red spider and mildew, and if these pests are not speedily destroyed you stand a very poor chance of getting any useful returns from your Vines. Amongst the chief causes of attack from red spider and mildew are the following : Over cropping the Vines in previous years ; insufficient thought and care in ventilating, especially in spring and early summer ; dryness at the roots, and a too close proximity of the foliage to the glass in hot weather. The cause of attack from thrips is usually the bringing of plants which are infested with them into the vinery. For the destruction of red spider and thrips you should fumigate with XL ALL on two successive evenings when the weather is calm, of course closing down the ventilators to prevent the escape of fumes. To destroy the mildew you should heat the hot water pipes moderately and paint the pipes over with flowers of sulphur made into the consistency of paint by added water, sealing up the vinery as closely as possible, as in the case of fumigating. Do this on two successive evenings of calm days. Afterwards do all you can to encourage healthy growth, by keeping up a moist and congenial atmosphere in the vinery.

Fumigating with Hydrocyanic Acid Gas

Q. White fly is a nuisance in my greenhouses. I am thinking of fumigating with hydrocyanic acid gas. In the directions it says : "After an hour the doors should be opened, also the ventilators. but only if they can be opened from the outside. In no circumstances should the house be entered until the next morning after ventilating." Most of my houses are span-roofed, with top ventilators and one at end. I could arrange to open the end one from outside, and, of course, the door. Would this be enough? How long would it be necessary to ventilate? Will white fly live all the winter in cold houses or frames?—*E. M., Chepstow.*

A. If you were to open the end ventilator all night it should be sufficient to clear the house of gas ; but it would be just as well to stand the door open for an hour in the morning. When using it I could only open the side ventilator of the houses, and I always found them clear in the morning. Great care should be exercised when using the above fumigant. The door of the house or houses should be securely fastened, and a notice on it warning anyone from entering the house ; *one inhalation of the gas will prove fatal.* If only troubled with white fly, I would advise fumigating with XL ALL compound, or any of the other good compounds offered for sale, as white fly is very easily killed. Of course, to get rid of it one must fumigate several times, as fresh broods hatch out. It is usually troublesome during autumn, and should not live during winter in houses or frames, unless they are kept hot and close The proportions I have used per 1,000 cubic feet are 2½ oz. cyanide of potassium, 4 oz. fluid sulphuric acid, 8 oz. water. Use a shallow earthenware vessel, and be careful to add the acid to the water, not the water to the acid.

CHAPTER IX

Fruit Growing Problems

Apple Trees Affected by Insects

Q. Will you inform me how to get rid of a pest which has infested about fifty of my young apple trees ? It appears at first white and fluffy, and when examined bugs are seen. They fasten on the

AN OLD ESPALIER APPLE TREE IN FULL BLOOM.

young growth and cause an ugly swelling on the bark, and eat right through the bark in places and cause the growth to die back. A gardener in this district told me to use soft soap, but I am sorry to say it has had little, if any, effect on them. I am afraid it only serves to drive them from one branch to another.— *Wm. Lawrence, Guildford.*

A. Your trees are infested by the American Blight (Schizoneura lanigera). In the autumn procure some ammoniacal liquid from the gasworks, and with a stiff brush well work the liquid into all cracks and indentations of the bark. Paraffin may be used. Very loose pieces of bark remove altogether. Having dealt with the branches and the trunk of the tree, carefully remove the soil from around the base of the trunk down to the roots, and treat it in a similar manner. Remove all the surface soil as far as the full spread of the branches, burn it, and put on some fresh loam in its place.

Grafted Apple Trees Dying

Q. Can you tell me the disease which has caused the death of enclosed Apple tree? I have grafted a good many trees the last year or two, many of them have been stricken in the same way.—*E., Kent.*

A. It is very seldom one hears of the death of an Apple tree grown under the usual natural conditions, but it is not at all unusual for grafted trees to succumb to the operation in the course of a year or two's time. This is more particularly the case with trees which are fairly old when grafted, the reason, we believe, being that the shock of cutting away the trees' limbs has so disorganised and weakened the trees' functions, both root and branch, that they have never recovered. We think that the death of your trees is due to this cause.

Transplanting an Apple Tree

Q. I moved an apple tree from one part of my garden to another on September 18th. All the leaves have shrivelled and appear dead. What can I do?— *W. H. C., Essex.*

A. It is a pity you moved the tree so early. You should have waited until the leaves had fallen and growth had ceased—say at the end of October or early in November—and the tree would scarcely have felt the check of removal. Being a young tree, we have no doubt it will soon get over any injury received. The symptoms you mention as regards the leaves dying and sticking on the branches, and the branches shrivelling, are the usual indication of too early lifting. Prune the tree about the end of December.

Pears Cracked and much Disfigured

Q. Can you tell me why my Pears are cracked and disfigured in this way? I enclose a few fruits.—*E. T. W., Slough.*

A. The fruits are infected by the disease known popularly as Pear scab, caused by the parasitic fungus, Fusicladium dendriticum var-

pirinum. This is probably the most general and widely distributed of fungoid diseases attacking Pears. The disease is usually only recognised on the fruit, the casual observer not noticing that the scab first appears on the leaves and young shoots, from whence the spores are washed by rain on to the fruit, which, as a rule, is the last to be attacked. If the fruit is nearly full grown before it is infected the spots formed by the fungus remain comparatively small and cracking does not generally ensue. As regards preventive and repressive treatment, the chief points to be attended to are : 1, all diseased fruits, or parings of them, should be collected and burned, and it is good practice to gather and burn the leaves as soon as they have fallen in the autumn, or bury them somewhat deeply in the ground. 2, spray the trees with a solution of sulphate of copper, 1 lb. of the sulphate to 25 gallons of water, or 1 oz. to $1\frac{1}{2}$ gallons. This should be applied during the winter. 3, spray with a solution of sulphide of potassium, dissolving 1 oz. of the sulphide in 1 gallon of hot water, and in another vessel $6\frac{1}{4}$ oz. of soft soap in a similar quantity of hot, soft water. When both thoroughly dissolve, add the latter solution to that of the sulphide of potassium, stir well, and dilute to $6\frac{1}{4}$ gallons with cold, soft water, mixing well. The spraying with the solution should be as follows : First, just as the flower buds begin to open ; second, when the petals of the flowers are falling ; and third, when the fruit is the size of Peas or slightly larger. If the season be rainy, a fourth treatment should be given twelve days after the third.

Pear Tree Cankered

Q. The enclosed Pear is from a tree about twenty or more years old, which is badly cankered. Can this be brought round to a healthy state ? It is now showing vigorous growth, but has suffered from neglect in the past. Will you kindly tell me good solutions with which to syringe large fruit trees for green fly, black fly, American blight ?—*Surrey Subscriber.*

A. The Pear tree may be improved by root pruning and the removal of a lot of surface soil. The latter must be replaced by new loam and a mulching of rotted manure. Cut off the cankered shoots quite close, and coat over the cut parts with Fir tree oil. To get rid of American blight, dress the tree with a solution of $\frac{1}{4}$ lb. of caustic soda dissolved in 1 quart of water, and 4 oz. of soft soap in a similar quantity ; add the two together, and then dilute with 5 gallons of rain water. The whole of the bark down to the roots of the trees must be thoroughly scrubbed with the mixture. Wear gloves while applying it. Quassia extract, used according to instructions, will kill the green and black aphides.

Plums Dropping before Ripening

Q. Many of the Plums on my trees are dropping this season before they are ripe. Can you explain this ?—*H. E. E., Maidstone.*

A. The fall of undersized fruits before they commence to colour is generally attributed to overcropping. It may also be due to the blossom being imperfectly fertilised, a condition brought about by the lack of bees or other insects which visit the early flowers. From the sample of soil and subsoil sent, we do not think that this is the cause of failure. We note that the tree was root pruned on one side last autumn ; if the tree has made a good deal of growth since then, we strongly advise you to root prune the other side this autumn and be sure that all large roots are cut, particularly those which go vertically downwards right underneath the base of the tree. Root pruning will oft-times bring an otherwise barren tree into bearing.

About Pruning Fruit Trees

Q. Please tell me why fruit trees cannot be pruned before the leaves fall.—*Fruit, Bedford.*

A. The reason why fruit trees ought not to be pruned before the foliage falls, is that by early pruning the tree would send out fresh shoots before the autumn had passed. These shoots would be useless as fruit spurs or as flowering wood, as they would be poorly developed and not ripened. Summer pruning consists of stopping the young growths in July.

Pears in Greenhouse Falling While Small

Q. The fruits are falling off my Pear trees (in greenhouse) in considerable numbers, although they are not half developed. Why is this ?—*H. E. B., Blackpool.*

A. The fruit is dropping on account of the imperfect fertilisation of the flowers. On cutting you will find that the young fruit is practically seedless. There are various causes accountable for this. Sometimes the pollen on the anthers of the flowers is weak and scanty, and lacking the power to fecundise the stigma. The remedy in this case is artificially to fertilise the flowers by applying the pollen to the stigma by the aid of a camel hair pencil. Too close and hot an atmosphere at the time the trees are in bloom will have the same effect, therefore always ventilate freely at this time in sunny weather. It is the same with the Apricot as the Pear. You will find the stone is jelly-like. You cannot keep the temperature too low whilst the Apricot is in bloom—say from 40° to 45° at night, with air all night and day.

Nectarines Splitting

Q. Many of my Nectarines on outdoor trees are badly split. Is it due to the wet summer?—*J. O. H., Weybridge.*

A. The excessive wet is most probably the cause. It is not an uncommon occurrence. Extreme drought owing to failure to supply

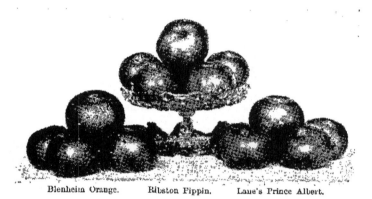

Blenheim Orange.   Ribston Pippin.   Lane's Prince Albert.

THREE GOOD APPLES.

the trees with sufficient water; saturation of the soil and overcropping all tend to induce the splitting of the fruits. Boards are sometimes placed on the borders to keep off heavy rains. Plums and Apricots are liable to be similarly affected.

Peach Leaf Blister

Q. Can you tell me the cause of my outdoor Peach tree leaves becoming badly blistered in April?—*E. W. W., Hastings.*

A. This is due to the attack of Peach curl or Blister fungus (Exoascus deformans) ; Cherries and Plums are also attacked by it. It is a troublesome disease, and until within the last few years no remedy has been found. However, a preparation called Medela, made by Messrs. G. Bunyard and Co., the Royal Nurseries, Maidstone, is said to be a certain cure.

Pruning Gooseberry Bushes

Q. Will you please tell me when is the proper time to prune Gooseberry bushes ?—*B. J. C., Melton Mowbray.*

A. The best time to prune Gooseberry bushes is in March, just before they start into growth, because birds during severe weather are very destructive to the buds. If they are pruned too early, there is a danger of the few buds left after pruning being destroyed. If all the branches are left on until spring, the birds are not so likely to do serious harm. If you have the means of protecting your trees from the birds, you may prune them any time between November and March.

Pruning Pear Trees

Q. My Pear trees bear little fruit, they are a mass of growth. Ought I to thin out the latter ?—*Anxious, Sale.*

A. There are too many small spurs bearing only leaf buds on your trees. These, when they are fully developed in summer, crowd the trees to such an extent that a minimum amount of sunshine, light, and air penetrates amongst the branches of the trees. As a consequence weak and unripe growth results, which cannot possibly produce remunerative crops of fruit. The best way of remedying this in your case is by disbudding. This means the act of rubbing away, with the finger and thumb, the weakest of the young shoots, which will appear on these spurs towards the end of April or the beginning of May, as soon as they are from $\frac{1}{4}$ to $\frac{1}{2}$ inch long. There will probably appear on each of the spurs from three to five of these young leaf growths ; in the case of the former, one, the weakest, should be rubbed off, and in the case of the latter, three of the weakest should be similarly rubbed off.

Myrobella Plum Hedge

Q. One side of my garden has a hedge formed of Myrobella Plum. Will you please inform me how to keep same trimmed so as not to take up too much room ?—*L. M., Catford.*

A. If the hedge in question is taking too much space, you may cut the side shoots back severely in the autumn, or not later than the end of February next. Young shoots will grow in spring, and these may be cut in in July.

Plum Tree Infested by Aphis

Q. I send you cuttings from a Plum tree to get your opinion of the malady and what you would recommend to cure. The whole tree is affected, and other trees in its neighbourhood are slightly contaminated by it.—*Coupar Angus.*

A. Your tree is badly affected by black aphis. The best way of destroying it is to cut away all the badly affected points of the young shoots and burn them, and then syringe your trees copiously with the following insecticide : Boil 2½ lb. of Quassia chips, and 1¾ lb. of soft soap, adding to them 25 gallons of water. This is a cheap and effective remedy for getting rid of aphis of all sorts. To make doubly sure of its destruction we should advise you to spray your trees in winter with the burning alkali wash. This will destroy all insect life it comes in contact with, without injury to the tree. It should be applied as soon as the trees are pruned in winter. This wash may be had of most seed merchants, with directions how to use.

Meaning of Freestone and Clingstone

Q. I often see these terms used in reference to Plums and Peaches. Can you explain ?—*T. O. A., Uxbridge.*

A. The term freestone means that the flesh parts cleanly from the stone when ripe. In clingstone varieties the opposite is the case. Old lime rubble or mortar rubbish will do very well to mix with the soil for fruit trees. Be careful not to over do it, however, especially if the ground is light.

Gumming in Stone Fruit Trees

Q. Some of my Cherry and Plum trees are not thriving ; the shoots exude a gummy substance. What can I do to cure them?—*Southerner, Hants.*

A. Most of us who possess or have the management of gardens know something about this disease, so far, at least, as its effect upon the trees is concerned. No fruit trees subject to it can have a long or prosperous life. There may be—probably there is—a predisposition to gumming in certain trees. The Moorpark Apricot is a notable sufferer, and I suppose, speaking generally, gumming is often caused by some injury to the branches, or a too free use of the knife. The fungus spores find a home where the bark is broken, and subsequently gum is seen to be exuding from the wound. A tight shred, by forcing the branch into contact with a nail, may break the bark and provide a genial home for the fungus. When gum is seen exuding from a branch or branches, if the tree is to be restored, cut out the infected part, and put on a poultice of cow manure, lime, soot, and clay, filling the wound with it, binding it on with a piece of cloth, and keeping the air from it until the wound has healed and filled up with new bark. Trees which are predisposed to gumming should be pruned chiefly in summer, and the knife as far as possible kept off them in the winter and spring. There are predisposing causes in cultivation, the most common being planting young trees in land which has been made too rich with manures.

Mulching Young Fruit Trees

Q. I have been told that it is a bad plan to manure the ground for young fruit trees at planting time. Is there any objection to giving manure afterwards? If not, how should it be applied?—*Amateur, Watford.*

A. Many people adopt the commendable practice of avoiding the use of any natural manure at all when they are planting their young trees in autumn or spring, for they fully appreciate the fact that there is already sufficient tendency to rampant growth without further encouraging it with stimulative materials. It is, however, most desirable to do something for the trees in the early summer which will encourage the roots to remain near the surface, instead of striking downwards into the cooler lower soil as soon as the weather becomes intensely hot and dry. To this end the grower should give as much water as may be necessary to moisten the soil to a depth of 3 feet or thereabouts, then fork over the surface and apply a 2-inch mulching of short manure. The food virtues of this will gradually find their way downwards, and the covering will tend to keep the surface cool and moist, and thus practically ensure the roots remaining near the top.

Cordon Gooseberries

Q. I have been recommended to plant cordon Gooseberries against a fence facing west. Do you advise my doing so?—*Grant, Dorking.*

A. Cordon Gooseberries fruit well either on north, south, east, or west fences. In fact, by planting a few on each aspect a welcome succession of fruit is obtained. Either single or multiple stemmed cordons may be chosen, the management of the plants does not present any serious difficulties. Summer pinching of the young shoots is necessary to admit light to the fruits and the buds on the stems, while the winter pruning will simply consist of hard cutting back to the two basal buds. Keep the surface loose and free from weeds, and maintain the supplies of available food by mulching in May with the finest natural manure that is at command.

C SHOWS POINT OF SUMMER PRUNING PEAR ; B POINT OF WINTER PRUNING.

AS A RESULT OF STOPPING THE SHOOT FURTHER GROWTHS WILL FORM AS AT A. THESE TOO ARE STOPPED WHEN A FEW INCHES LONG. PRUNE BACK TO B IN WINTER.

Unfruitful Strawberries

Q. My Strawberry plants have far too many leaves on them, and the leaves are too big. Can you give me any idea of the reason for this? Many of the plants did not flower, and the others had not much fruit.—*S. A. G., Croydon.*

A. Your large, unfruitful plants of Strawberries have probably been layers taken from others which were unfruitful. Destroy them and plant fresh runners in August or early September. Strawberry layers should only be taken from plants that are fruitful.

Raspberries Unsatisfactory

Q. My Raspberry canes (which were planted sixteen years ago) have borne very little fruit this summer, and the new growths for

J

next year's crop are also disappointing. Every autumn I have stirred the surface soil very slightly and then laid on a fairly large quantity of stable manure. Is it possible that I have given them too much of this ?—*Canes, Hawick.*

A. Your Raspberry plants are very old, and the best thing you can do is to make a new plantation. The medium sized young canes from your old plantation may be used for the new one, but it would be more satisfactory to purchase new canes. The old plants may be retained for one more year until the new ones are remunerative. In the meantime allow the manure to lie on the surface, and do not dig it in either this autumn or in spring. The pruning of Raspberries is simple. The fruit is produced on the previous year's growth; thus the shoots that have fruited are cut out as soon as the fruit is gathered. The young growths are, of course, taken care of and tied up; they will fruit the next year.

Gathering Pears

Q. Can you give me a few hints on gathering Pears ?—*Amateur, S. Wales.*

A. Test the fruits by gently lifting, when if they part easily from the trees it may usually be safely taken as a sign of readiness for gathering, though not for eating. Late sorts should be allowed to hang as long as possible; premature gathering of these will cause them to shrivel and be tough and leathery in texture, devoid of juiciness and flavour.

The Loganberry

Q. We are thinking of planting the Loganberry here, but as our soil is very heavy, with yellow clay subsoil, would you inform me if you think it would do in this soil ?—*Sutton, Surrey.*

A. Yes; you may plant the Loganberry in the heavy soil; the plants will succeed very well. But it is advisable, of course, to trench the ground, and thoroughly break up the subsoil, leaving it below, however. The Loganberry grows vigorously in good soil, and is an admirable plant for covering unsightly fences, ugly corners, etc., or it may be trained as an espalier. It fruits best when the branches are spread out. The pruning is similar to that needed by the Raspberry. Cut out the old growths as soon as they have fruited, and train in the new to fruit the following year. The best fruits are produced by canes of the previous summer's growth : removing the old shoots encourages the development of new ones.

Red Currants Failing

Q. I have sent you a few leaves of my Red Currants, also a small box of fruit. Would you please tell me how I can prevent their getting so black? The leaves first get in a sticky state and then turn black just as if soot had been thrown over them. Do you think smuts from chimneys would cause it? We have a brick kiln near.— *J., Bradford.*

A. In the first place your Currant tree leaves have been infested

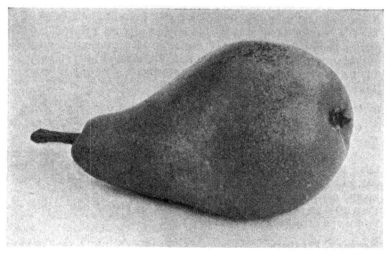

PEAR DURONDEAU.

badly with aphides, and the matter from them has covered the leaves with a sticky substance which has been favourable to the collection of dust, and soot from the brick kiln. The only thing you can do is to syringe the bushes early in the season and free the foliage from the aphides, and frequently afterwards to dislodge the dust and soot.

Black Currants Affected with Big Bud

Q. Can you tell me how to cure my Black Currants of this most troublesome pest?—*Anxious, Esher.*

A. Since the trees are young, having been planted only two years, it would be rather unwise to uproot them all on account of the big bud. A better plan is to cut them all hard back now (April). Cut each infested shoot down to within a few inches of the ground, and remove by hand any suspiciously large buds as they appear. After this hard pruning, which at this season will mean the loss of a year's crop, dust the bushes with a mixture of lime and sulphur, and repeat the application after an interval of two weeks. Next spring dust again with lime and sulphur, using 1 part unslaked lime to 2 parts flowers of sulphur. Thoroughly dust the bushes over when they are wet, and continue to do so every few weeks until the middle of May. After pruning carefully collect all the prunings and burn them. Yes ; it is quite likely that the old bushes will be affected since the disease is now present in your garden. As a preventive dust the bushes over with the lime and sulphur mixture and pick off any buds unduly swollen. If you intend to propagate new plants from cuttings be sure to do so from a clean stock.

Gathering and Storing Filberts

Q. Please say how Filbert Nuts should be stored.—*E. W. W., Kent.*

A. The Nuts should be obtained on a fine dry day, not separating them from the husks. We have found it a good plan to lay them out on mats and sacks for a few days ; they are then readily picked up and carried to shelter at night or should rain set in. Afterwards, they may be stored in jars or boxes, or be spread out evenly and thinly upon the floor of a cool, dry shed.

Keeping Medlars

Q. Will you tell me the best way to keep and ripen Medlars ?— *J. Astridge, Hants.*

A. Gather the fruits before they are frozen on the trees, and store them on shelves in a cool, airy room where they will soften and become fit for use. You only need guard against damp and decay of the fruits.

Replanting Raspberries

Q. I have a large stock of canes which have been allowed to run riot. They have grown over 8 feet high, and though there is every indication of a good supply of fruit we have not been able to get a handful from the complete row of over 80 feet run. I thought of transplanting them this year to a new situation and of making them form a screen round a plot which I propose to make into a fruit garden. Do you recommend this, and how can I proceed so as to make them form such a screen ?—*T. E., Mitcham.*

A. Yes ; the Raspberries would do well planted to form a screen round the fruit quarter in the garden. The planting should be done in November. Select canes of medium strength and discard the gross and weakly ones. Dig the soil deeply and put in some rotted manure, and after planting is done put on a good surface mulch of littery manure. The canes should be planted about 9 inches apart. Black Currants do best in a cool position ; the Red and White varieties require an open, sunny place.

How to Keep Walnuts

Q. Would you kindly inform me as to the best way to keep Walnuts when they are ripe, so as to have them good for some length of time ?—*A. S., Surrey.*

A. When the Nuts are ripe, spread them out thinly just long enough to get the shells dry, then place them in bottles or jars, and securely cork the latter. Store the bottles or jars in a cool, dry cupboard.

Q. Referring to the above question. As we have rather a large quantity this season, would tins such as biscuit tins answer the purpose if they were fastened down securely ? We put some in a large pot with a piece of thick tin for a cover and buried them in the earth floor of the potting shed, but they did not keep. Was it because they were too damp or not sufficiently airtight ?—*A. Scrivener, Bucks.*

A. Yes ; if you can seal up the biscuit tins the Nuts may be kept in them. The Nuts, buried in the earth as you state, would rot, unless they had been first dried and then kept in airtight vessels.

Blackberries for the Garden

Q. I am anxious to grow Blackberries. Should I plant the common kind, or are there better sorts ?—*Ignoramus, Bath.*

A. So widely are excellent Blackberries appreciated that one cannot help feeling surprised that they are not far more extensively planted in gardens. They do not involve either a great deal of space or a considerable amount of skilled attention, and the crops of fruit which they bear annually will be more than welcome. I should advise planters to beware of the majority of American varieties, for some of the seedlings of our own country are superior in every respect. A really good form of the Parsley Leaved Bramble cannot be beaten, but apart from this selected wildings are the things to choose. Planted in deeply dug and generously manured ground in November, watered with liquid manure freely after perfect establishment, and mulched with good manure each winter, they will thrive and crop grandly for years. Practically the only attention demanded in the way of cutting is to remove all old shoots for which there is not room after the fruit is gathered.

Morello Cherry

Q. Is this a profitable fruit to grow on walls ?—E. W., Hendon.

A. The Morello Cherry is valuable for covering the walls of cottages, on which it hardly ever fails to produce good crops. It will thrive on a wall facing north. The fruits sell well, as they come in after the glut of other fruit is over. This Cherry grows and produces well on any aspect, and the simplest kind of training suits it best. Plant healthy, fan-trained trees, and let them spread out evenly in all directions. Keep them clean during the growing season by dusting with tobacco powder or syringing with tobacco water, dipping the points of the young shoots into the mixture. Cover with nets to keep off birds, so as to let the fruits get fully ripe. In winter cut out weakly and exhausted fruit, and nail in the young shoots of the preceding summer's growth full length, as the Morello bears the finest fruit on the young wood.

Pruning Roots of Pear Trees

Q. I should like your advice about two Pear trees which I have. They are wall trees facing west and south-west, very vigorous, and plenty of bloom every year and set fruits, but when these get about the size of Peas they fall off. Every year this happens I get no fruit. This has been going on for nine years. They always bloom the second time each season, and seeing your article on root pruning I thought I would try the operation. I took out a trench 2 feet deep, about 3 feet away from the stem, half way round the tree, but could not find any roots to prune; the roots seem to strike down into the subsoil close to the wall. I could not find any short fibrous roots near the surface at all. If you could advise me on the subject I should feel grateful.—S. C., Devonport.

A. We are rather surprised you did not find any roots after digging 2 feet deep at 3 feet from the stem of a tree nine years old. Possibly they have gone under the wall to the other side. If you can get at the other side, try to find them there. If this cannot be done, the next best thing to do is to open out the trench again, digging it 1 foot deeper and clearing all the soil out. You must then tunnel under the tree until you come to the main tap roots, which you will find not far from a direct line of the stem of the tree. Cut them through and leave in the ground. Fill in the space tunnelled, ramming the soil hard, and we hope the effect will be to bring your trees round to fruit bearing condition.

Standard Fruit Trees for Sandy Soil

Q. I have a small space in my garden in which I wish to put standard fruit trees ; the soil is pure sand. I have had holes 5 feet square and 3 feet deep dug, into which I intend putting soil and manure. It is on the north slope of the hill. I have room for seventeen trees 9 feet apart, and would be very glad if you could advise me what trees I ought to have. I thought of having Apples, Pears, Plums, and Cherries if I could get them suitable for the ground. I want them all for dessert fruit, not cooking, if possible.—*Spindrift, Farnham.*

A. The following varieties of the different kinds of fruit you require we hope will suit you well. They are strong growing, fruitful sorts. Six Apples, all dessert : Mr. Gladstone, ripe July and August ; Lady Sudeley, September ; James Grieve, October ; Cox's Orange Pippin, November to Christmas; Allington Pippin, December and January ; Allen's Everlasting, January to March. Four Pears, all dessert: Williams' Bon Chrétien, September ; Louise Bonne of Jersey, October ; Emile d'Heyst, November ; Doyenné du Comice, December. Four Plums: Reine Claude de Bavay (Gage), Old Green Gage, Kirk's, Transparent Gage. Three Cherries : Kentish Bigarreau, Guigne d'Annonay, Governor Wood.

Cherry for West Fence

Q. Which is a good eating Cherry to grow on tarred boards, aspect west, soil gravel and clay ?—*G. E., Sussex.*

A. Frogmore Bigarreau, light, and Black Tartarian, dark, are suitable sorts.

Three Late Keeping Apples

Q. Which three late keeping Apples are most suitable for an orchard as standards, soil gravel and clay ?—*G. E., Sussex.*

A. Newton Wonder, Bramley's Seedling, and King Edward VII.

Manure for Strawberries

Q. I have been advised to dress Strawberry beds heavily with stable manure. This I have not, but have a good quantity of fowl manure. Would this do as well if used in smaller quantities?—*J. H., Devon.*

A. Littery manure is put on as a mulch to protect the roots as well as to feed the plants. Fowl manure would not answer the purpose as well, though you may apply it at the rate of 1 bushel per square rod of ground in spring. It would feed the plants, but not protect them much.

Cuttings of Gooseberries and Red and White Currants

Q. I understand Gooseberries and Currants are readily increased from cuttings. Will you me tell how to prepare these?—*Amateur, Berks.*

A. Cuttings are made in October from the past summer's growth. Like Rose cuttings, they should be about 12 inches in length, but it is essential to cut out all the buds with the exception of about four of the uppermost, from which the bush is produced. Were the others left they would be a constant source of annoyance from the suckers they would certainly produce. Insert the cuttings similarly to those of Roses. In making Black Currant cuttings the lower buds are not cut out.

FRUITS UNDER GLASS

Nectarines Shrivelling

Q. I enclose herewith a Nectarine. Will you tell me the cause of its shrivelling and, in many cases, the cause of the non-stoning of the fruit? The tree is well established in an unheated leanto Peach house. Also, what should be the night temperature of the house after the blossoms have set?—*Ignorant, Hampshire.*

A. The Nectarines have been mildewed when they were in a green state, and it is the cause of the fruit's decay now. The soil is deficient in lime, and in consequence the fruit did not stone properly. After the fruits have set, a night temperature of 60° will be sufficient.

Peaches Stringy

Q. Could you tell me the cause of Peaches getting stringy towards the stone?—*C. D., Cheshire.*

A. We think that this is a question of the varieties of Peaches you may happen to grow, as the Clingstone varieties often have this failing. You say that your trees are very healthy, and the fruits very fine, therefore the stringiness cannot be the fault of the cultural treatment.

Fertilising Melon Flowers

Q. I understand that the female flowers of Melons have to be fertilised ; could you tell me how to tell the female flowers and how to fertilise them ?—*G. V. W., Cheshire.*

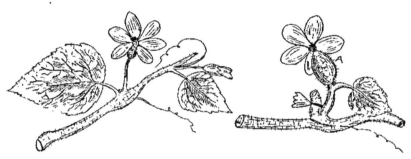

GROWTH OF MELON SHOWING MALE OR POLLEN FLOWER.

MELON SHOOT SHOWING FEMALE FLOWER. NOTE THE EMBRYO FRUIT AT A.

A. You will readily recognise the female flowers of the Melon by the embryo fruit at the base, and by the absence of anthers (bearing pollen), while the male flowers bear anthers only, no stigma. To fertilise the female blossoms, pluck a male flower and apply the pollen from the anthers to the stigma of the former. The best time to do this is about midday. The atmosphere is then likely to be dry ; a dry air is necessary to fertilisation. In wet, dull weather Melon fruits often fail to "set" or form.

Pears and Plums under Glass

Q. I have a Peach house, facing south, with a high wall, and I should like to grow some Cordon Pears and Plums on the back, as it is not a very good district for growing fruit outside. If you think it is a suitable position, I should be glad if you would name a few varieties.—*W. W., Walsall.*

A. Yes; you may grow Cordon Pears and Plum trees on the back wall of your Peach house successfully, if you do not force them too hard. Marie Louise Marie Louise d'Uccle, Souvenir du Congrès, Durondeau, Pitmaston Duchess, Doyenné du Comice, Louise Bonne of Jersey, and Williams' Bon Chrétien, Pears; and Denniston's Superb, Green Gage, Jefferson, Kirke's, and Transparent Gage Plums may be planted. It is impossible to force Plums and Pears as Grapes, Peaches and Nectarines may be forced. They will not succeed in a high temperature. Until the fruits are formed an average temperature of 50˚ is high enough, afterwards it may be increased to 60˚.

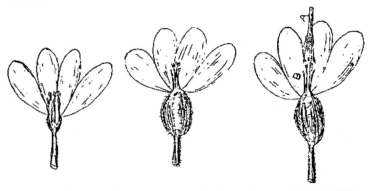

MALE AND FEMALE FLOWERS OF THE MELON.   THE LATTER ARE EASILY DISTINGUISHED BY THE EMBRYO FRUIT BELOW THE PETALS.   THE THIRD FIGURE SHOWS HOW POLLI-NATION IS CARRIED OUT.

Cherries and Tomatoes Grown in Same House

Q. Can Cherries be forced profitably so as to get the house cleared by the end of May? to be followed by Tomatoes that have been brought on in 5-inch pots in another house.—*G. W. T., Staffs.*

A. Cherries in pots can be successfully forced to produce Cherries from the first to the last week in May. The plants should be brought under glass the first week in December; started in low temperature (40°), and forced very slowly without exciting the trees until the fruit is set, when more heat, up to 60°, may be applied. Governor Wood, Early Rivers, Frogmore Bigarreau, and Black Tartarian are suitable sorts.

Nectarines Splitting

Q. Can you say why my Nectarines grown under glass have split badly ?—*G. E. H., Worcester.*

A. The cause of the Nectarines splitting is insufficient ventilation during hot weather. Temperatures under glass rise in consequence, causing so great an acceleration in the flow of sap as partly to congest the arteries through which it flows. Hence an overflow, and the consequent splitting of the fruit. Remedy : Reduce the temperature by free ventilation night and day whilst the hot weather lasts. You may safely let the temperature drop to 50° Fah. or lower at night ; in the middle of the day, with sun heat and plenty of air in the house, it may rise to 80° or 85° for a few hours.

On Growing Cucumbers

Q. I am anxious to be able to gather Cucumbers in April. Will they need a hotbed, and when should I sow the seed ?—*E. J. K., Enfield.*

A. First get together suitable material for filling the pits. The best material for keeping up a steady heat is that composed of freshly gathered up leaves and short stable manure mixed well together and turned several times in an open shed, previous to filling the Cucumber pit. Sowing the seed in small pots early in January is the plan usually adopted, as this ensures no check in potting on. Use soil fairly damp and plunge in the hotbed, giving no water until germination takes place. When the third true leaf appears they may be planted out into mounds of rich soil. Syringe the plants frequently with tepid water, and see that a constant and sufficient heat is maintained. A night temperature of 60 -65 is best, rising 10 during the day without sun heat. Keep free from draughts. Cucumbers require a warm atmosphere with little ventilation.

CHAPTER X

Trees and Shrubs

Self Clinging Climbers

Q. Will you please give me a list of self clinging climbers, other than Ivy, suitable for a cement wall facing south ?—*S. H. P., Belfast.*

A. The following are suitable : Hydrangea petiolaris, Vitis semi-cordata, and of course Ampelopsis Veitchi. The choice of self clinging climbers, excluding Ivy, is very limited, but these three are good growers and thrive in most places.

Planting Bed of Flowering Shrubs

Q. I enclose a rough sketch of bed 24 feet long, 12 feet wide, with wall 3 feet high at back facing east, well sheltered by house and buildings. Will you advise the best flowering shrubs and bush Roses to grow for garden decoration intermixed with hardy annuals, and, finally, bedding out plants ? I wish to make a tennis lawn on south-west side of wall, but I want to hide it from the other part of the garden without having the shrubs too high and cumbersome. Will you also advise how to plant ? I should like bush Roses of the Sweet Briar class, but do not wish to confine myself to that class alone.—*Beginner, Blandford.*

A. Taking the part of the house nearest the bed, we should plant the following shrubs and Roses, which would occupy a width say of about 6 feet. Commencing near the Bay tree, plant Genista andreanus, Rose Aglaia, Philadelphus grandiflorus, Veronica Traversii, Lilac Madame Lemoine, Spartium junceum, Rose Hiawatha on stump or pole. Then, starting 3 feet away from these plants, Rose Blush Rambler, standard Pyrus Malus floribunda, Hybrid Sweet Briar Lady Penzance, Buddleia veitchiana, Hybrid Sweet Briar Anne of Geierstein, standard double flowering Cherry Jas. H. Veitch, Forsythia suspensa, Rose Rubin. Towards the outer side of bed, starting near Rose Blush Rambler, plant Weigela E. Rathke, Rose Goldfinch, Rose Conrad F. Meyer Spiraea A. Waterer, Rose, Tausendschon, Guelder Rose, Hybrid Sweet Briar, Amy Robsart, Rose Gruss an Teplitz, Rose Leuchtstern, Pyrus Malus angustifolia.

Should you want a few slow growing subjects to finish off with plant Yucca flaccida, double flowering Gorse, Fuchsia Riccartoni. Caryopteris Mastacanthus, and Hibiscus Lotus albus. Allow the Roses to grow as free bushes, and do not crowd any of the plants, rather leave some out altogether. One cannot quite definitely say how to arrange unless one is on the spot, but this is a general idea.

Evergreen Shrubs to Grow Beneath Austrian Pine

Q. Can you tell me if there is any evergreen shrub that will thrive beneath an Austrian Pine?—*E. H. T., Southampton.*

A. The best evergreen shrubs to grow beneath Austrian Pines are Rhododendron ponticum, Aucuba japonica, Berberis Aquifolium, Periwinkle, St. John's Wort (Hypericum calycinum), and common Ivy. The Pine leaves are detrimental to many shrubs, but the above plants succeed fairly well, more especially when the leafage is not very dense.

Shrubs and Plants for Border Facing North

Q. Please give a list of shrubs and plants suitable for north border.—*M. S. S., Hazlemere.*

A. Aucuba, Laurustinus, Euonymus, Lilac (Syringa), Laurel, Deutzia, Spiraea (S. aruncus being very suitable), Campanula, Anemone, Sunflower, Veronica, Michaelmas Daisies, Gaillardia, Delphinium, herbaceous Phloxes and Funkia, tuberous Begonia, Fuchsia, Phlox Drummondii, Mignonette, Stocks, Asters, Marigolds, and Marguerites are suitable.

Plants to form Strong Fence

Q. I am about to put a fence around a plot of ground intended for garden, and I thought of planting a Myrobalan Plum for a quick growing and an almost impregnable fence. Should be glad if you will give your opinion on the following: Would it be wise to mix the Myrobalan Plum with Privet or not? Would it add to beautifying the place if fronting the road was planted with say Hornbeam or Hornbeam and Privet mixed, or same as above? Do you advise Holly for the front, say bushes about 2½ feet in height?—*W. M., Lynn.*

A. Myrobella Plum and Privet would form a very good fence or hedge. Put in three plants of the former and then one of the latter. Yes; Holly would do splendidly for a front fence. Put in the plants zigzag fashion and about 15 inches apart from plant to plant.

Pruning Deutzia

Q. This flowering shrub has been very beautiful in my garden, but I am at a loss as to how to prune it. Please advise.—*R. A. M., King's Lynn.*

A. All that is necessary is to thin out to the base feeble and weak growths where they are crowded, and to leave the plant in such a condition that it appears shapely. This may be done as soon as it has finished flowering. If you cut it hard down, as you propose doing, it would simply give rise to an abundance of young and useless growth.

On Planting Trees

Q. I should be glad of your advice as to the proper method of planting trees. Which is the best Pine to plant to form a screen? —*Midland.*

A. Since the soil is a tenacious clay and presumably not well drained, the stations in which the trees are to be planted should be dug out to a depth of $2\frac{1}{2}$ or 3 feet; the width of the stations should be in proportion to the trees or shrubs to be planted; in your soil they cannot be too large. Place broken bricks at the bottom, and follow with lime rubble and rough turf. Plant the trees to their previous depth, and carefully spread out all the roots before covering in the soil. If possible, some good, coarse, turfy loam should be introduced with the garden soil at the time of planting, but the soil which immediately covers the roots should be fine. One of the best Pines to form a screen is the Corsican Pine, Pinus Laricio; it is of rapid growth, and rabbits and hares are said not to interfere with it. In planting Pines and Lombardy Poplars to form a screen they should be placed rather closely together, so that the alternate trees may be removed after a year or two. The distance apart depends entirely upon the size of the trees at the time they leave the nurseryman's hands. In addition to the Lombardy Poplar and the Corsican Pine, the following are suitable to form a screen or wind break : Hornbeam, Larch, Austrian Pine, and Douglas Spruce.

When to Transplant Shrubs

Q. Please tell me the best time to transplant the shrubs mentioned.—*H. W. K., Catford.*

A. Rhododendrons and Azaleas can be transplanted with safety in early April, and we should advise you to defer the operation until that season. The Mock Orange, Berberis, and Clerodendron may all be removed in October. Transplanting will not delay the time of flowering of your strong growing Clerodendron trichotomum ; it is more likely to induce it to flower. Lilies may be lifted in October and stored in dry silver sand for the winter in a frostproof shed.

Planting Ampelopsis

Q. I should be much obliged if you could tell me the best time to plant Ampelopsis Veitchi and any special cultural hints.—*A. E. B., Watford.*

A. The best time to plant is in early November or late October, although planting may be carried out between October and the end of March when the weather is mild. This plant is of the simplest cultivation, and all you have to do is to attach the shoots to the wall to give it a start.

Hedge Round Garden

Q. I am thinking of planting a hedge round my cottage garden, I want one that will grow strong and quickly. I thought perhaps Privet would be most suitable.—*C. G. B., Basingstoke.*

A. You would probably find Privet the best plant for your purpose. It will make a good hedge sooner than anything else. Make sure you get the oval-leaved Privet (Ligustrum ovalifolium). Hornbeam makes a good hedge and is fairly quick growing, while Quick or Thorn has much to recommend it.

About Clematis, Quick Growing Plant, and Low Hedge

Q. What quick growing plant would you recommend for hiding cottage bedroom windows overlooking vegetable garden ? What would make a nice low hedge in front of drawing room and facing drive gate ? Last spring we planted two Clematises, Jackmani superba and Gipsy Queen, to trail on pillars of verandah in drive. The former grew quickly to about 7 feet and ready to blossom, when suddenly it began to droop and died downwards.—*Mrs. Adams, Bucks.*

A. Clematis plants thrive best in a naturally dry situation, and in a fairly light soil. The plants do sometimes die down suddenly, owing to some check. The young shoots may grow up and prove successful. Ceanothus azureus Gloire de Versailles bears long spikes of lavender blue flowers from midsummer to late autumn. It would be a charming substitute. Cupressus macrocarpa would quickly grow and form a screen ; and the oval-leaved Privet or Euonymus or Daisy Bush, Olearia Haasti, would prove satisfactory as a low hedge.

Pruning Clematis montana

Q. The house that I have leased has a very old Clematis montana growing over porch in front. ·When I first saw the house this was a mass of white bloom, but underneath the bloom was a thick mass of dead wood, which I thought most objectionable. When doing up the house all this had to be cut away, now the front of the house is covered with long trails. I am told there will be no blossom next year if I trim these long trails, but I cannot have them hanging all over the place, yet I should like to have the blossom.—*M. de K., Bournemouth.*

A. C. montana requires quite different treatment from C. Jackmani, as the former flowers next year on the growths made this year. If you wish for flowers next year you must leave this year's young growths. Cut back the plant each year as soon as the flowers are over. C. Jackmani is in flower now (August) on the growths made this spring and early summer.

Pruning Ivy

Q. Please tell me how to proceed when pruning Ivy on wall. When should I prune?—*E. M. H., Ashbourne.*

A. The specimen you send is one of the large-leaved Ivies, called Hedera Helix Amurensis. You may prune it in March, and it can be cut back fairly hard so as to get it back to the wall. Subsequent prunings may take place twice a year, spring and summer, to keep it within bounds, the spring pruning being severe and the second or summer pruning in July light. In the former case it may be cut well back to the wall, whilst in the latter case the long, loose shoots only should be shortened. It is usually advisable to use a knife instead of shears for the large leaved Ivies, for if leaves are mutilated they are very unsightly.

Evergreens for Hedge

Q. Can you advise as to planting an evergreen shrub for a division line position, north side of house shaded by an Ash tree, height to be kept to 2 feet? Would Butcher's Broom (Ruscus aculeatus) be suitable? if so, would it be too late to plant now (November)? and what distance apart should you plant to form a continuous row? I want to keep clear of Privet.—*F. M., Leicester.*

A. The plant you suggest, Butcher's Broom (Ruscus aculeatus),

RHODODENDRON LORD PALMERSTON, ROSY CRIMSON.

will be suitable for the position you mention. The distance apart to place the plants will depend entirely on their size, but from 9 to 12 inches would be a suitable distance for average sized plants. Other useful shrubs for such a position are Gaultheria Shallon and Berberis (Mahonia) Aquifolium. The latter is an easily obtained plant, does very well in shade, and stands cutting back well. November is a good month for planting.

Transplanting a Holly 12 feet High

Q. Might I safely undertake the transplantation of a Holly 12 feet high? If so, when should the work be done?—*M. M., Herts.*

A. It is quite possible safely to transplant a Holly 12 feet high, but it must be done carefully. The work should be done either in September or early May. You will need to move a large ball of earth with it, especially if it is a very old specimen. Two men will be required to get the plant ready to transplant—that is to work round the ball and tie it up tightly in stout canvas, undermine it, and place two pieces of plank beneath the centre—and prepare the new position. If it is only to be moved a short distance a trench can be made from one hole to the other, and four or five men will be able to do the work by means of planks and rollers. If, however, it has to be moved some distance it will have to be rolled out of the hole by means of an inclined plane and rolled into the new one by the same means ; this would require eight to ten men, according to the size of the ball.

Evergreen Shrubs for Garden

Q. Please name shrubs that will keep green all the winter, say, for ordinary soil near house. What shrubs can you recommend for planting soon (October)?—*E. S., Beckenham.*

A. The following shrubs would do well with you, and keep green all the winter. Aucuba japonica, Berberis stenophylla, B. (Mahonia) Aquifolium, Tree Ivies, Rhododendron ponticum and any of the garden varieties, variegated Box, Olearia Haastii, and Laurustinus. The latter may be damaged if a very severe winter is experienced, but it usually grows again from the bottom. All may be planted at once. The two best for a shady place are Aucuba japonica and Berberis Aquifolium. Any ordinary garden soil is suitable for these shrubs except the Rhododendrons. These can only be grown in places where lime is not found in any great quantity, although they do not need peat as commonly supposed.

ONE OF THE MOST HANDSOME OF THE SPIRAEAS (ARIAEFOLIA).

Sowing Seeds of and Pruning Forest Trees

Q. Please give me information about the sowing of seeds of Larch, Oak, Ash, Beech, the time to collect the seeds, and the time to prune Ash, Oak, and Beech.—*W. J. B., Norfolk.*

A. Larch, Oak, and Beech seeds may be collected in early October. Ash should be collected in August. Oak and Beech ought to be sown in October in nursery beds 4 feet wide. If you are troubled by mice, roll the seeds in red lead before sowing. Larch seeds may be either sown in October or kept until spring. If kept until the latter time store in a cool room. As Oaks lose their vitality very quickly if allowed to become dry, store them in damp sand if you are unable to sow when gathered. Ash seeds may be sown as soon as collected. Oak, Beech, and Ash trees may be pruned any time between the beginning of June and end of December, but not during the spring and late winter months. If the trees are planted under proper forest conditions they ought to require no other pruning than the snipping off of a rival leader, for, by close planting, the trunks clean themselves. If you are going to prune large trees, be careful to make the cuts well up to the trunk and tar the wounds over as soon as made.

Raising a Stock of Evergreens

Q. I should be glad if you would tell me how I can raise a stock of evergreen plants for shrubbery planting.—*E. T. H., Willesden.*

A. October is probably the best month of the year for the propagation of hardy evergreen shrubs by means of cuttings. Protection is unnecessary, yet a frame is very useful when choice varieties have to be dealt with, as they root more readily with this assistance. Choose pieces from 6 inches to 1 foot in length and remove the lower leaves. A north border that is slightly protected is the best position for them, and they should be inserted to about two thirds their length, placing a little sand in the bottom of the trench to assist root formation. Make quite firm, and if after severe frost any are lifted they should be trodden down immediately ; the lifting power that frost possesses is remarkable. Rough winds will also cause damage if the cuttings are not kept firm. Where a frame is used this precaution is to a certain extent unnecessary, but it is well to look over them after a spell of hard frost. Among the shrubs which may be propagated thus are common Laurel, Aucuba, Privet, Box, Choisya ternata (in the south), Euonymus, etc.

CHAPTER XI

Home Grown Vegetables

Storing Carrots and Turnips

Q. Please instruct me how to store Carrots and Turnips properly. I have lost many through improper storage.--*A.S. T., Edinburgh.*

A. On the approach of severe weather, that is generally during October, the Carrots should be very carefully lifted, some of the superabundant earth removed, the tops neatly cut off, and the roots stored in sacks with the heads outwards, filling in the crevices and covering with sand. They may also be stored in clamps out of doors in the manner often practised with Potatoes. Or they may be stored in a frostproof shed in layers with straw between each layer. The Turnips would be better used as they are lifted, but they may be kept for a time, in the manner advised for Carrots, in a frostproof shed.

On Growing Cardoons]

Q. I should be glad of some help in the matter of growing the Cardoon, a vegetable I am fond of, but which is greatly neglected. —*J. U., Monmouth.*

A. We do not recommend you to try to propagate the Cardoon from the shoots sent up from the roots, as it is so readily raised from seed sown after the winter has passed. Seed should be sown in the places where the plants are to be grown. Sow the seed in little bunches about 18 inches apart in rows 4 feet apart. The plants can then be thinned to one at each station, and in due time secured to stakes. Blanching should take place when full growth is attained, *i.e.* during August. It takes about two months to blanch properly. If you wish to save time you could sow seed under glass in May and, after planting out, adopt the French method of covering each plant with straw thatched from the bottom to the top around each plant. A small ridge of soil is drawn to the foot, and blanching is perfected in about a month. The Cardoon does not meet with the favour in Britain with which it is regarded on the Continent, where the stalks and midribs of the inner leaves are esteemed in soups and salads.

Clubbing among Vegetables, Application of Lime

Q. Cabbages and other vegetables of the Brassica family are badly attacked by club. I thought of applying lime to the soil to improve matters. Is this right? if so, how much should I apply?— *H. A. B., Newport.*

A. You are certainly contemplating the right thing, for nothing will tend to check the ravages of this widespread disease more than lime. Scatter freshly slaked lime all over the surface of the soil in October or November. On a large scale it may be used with good effect from 5 to 7 tons per acre. The lime should be dug into the ground after the lapse of two or three days. Do not apply the lime so near to the fruit trees that it is brought in direct contact with the roots when digging in.

Young Marrows Failing to Develop

Q. Can you tell me why Vegetable Marrows, when 1 inch or 2 inches long, refuse to grow any bigger and are worthless?— *E. W. M., Chester.*

A. The reason for the young Marrows turning yellow and damping off when about 1 inch or 2 inches in length is their not being fertilised. The Marrow plant produces two kinds of flowers —the female which bears the Marrow fruit, and the male which pollinates the female. If the female flowers are not pollinated, they are in consequence unfertilised and therefore undeveloped. As a rule bees are responsible for the pollination of Marrow flowers; in order that bees and other insects should perform this work it is very necessary that the male flowers should not be removed, for it sometimes happens that the male flowers are picked off under the wrong impression that they are false blooms and of no use to the plant. The very damp and much colder weather which we have had may also have a good deal to do with the Marrows failing to set their fruits.

Club Disease in Cabbages

Q. Please tell me what causes these knotted lumps on Cabbages. My crop is badly attacked by this disease. The leaves are much eaten by caterpillars.—*W. S. T., Malvern.*

A. The plants are affected by club disease and attacked by the grubs of the Cabbage butterfly at the same time. As soon as you can manage to do it the allotment should be given a heavy dressing of lime, for this is the best known agent to ward off the club root disease of Cabbages, Turnips, and similar crops. It would be as well to grow Potatoes, Onions, or other crops, and to give all the Brassicas a change, since they are so liable to be attacked on your soil. It is quite possible that the plants were attacked at the time of planting out. They should be examined at planting time, and if affected the roots should be puddled in a mixture of paraffin, soft soap, and soot water.

Liming Ground for Potatoes

Q. Please assist me in the following. I have a plot of garden ground (26 poles), to which I intend giving lime. The soil is medium stiff. What quantity would you advise me to give it? The best time to put on, now (autumn) or spring? Whether to dig or fork it in? I am to crop it with Potatoes again.—*Constant Reader, Montrose.*

A. Deeply dig your plot, leaving the soil rough on the surface. Then apply 2 pecks of slaked lime (in powder form) per rod of ground. Scatter the powdered lime evenly on the surface, and let it remain so for a few weeks, then fork it in.

Asparagus

Q. Can I water Asparagus beds with sea water, and frequently or otherwise?—*R. B., I. of W.*

A. Seaweed in moderation is a good manure to use in the making of new Asparagus beds, but we have never known or heard of beds being watered with sea water. Unless very greatly diluted, the result of using it, we think, would be disastrous to the Asparagus plants. Asparagus plants thrive best when kept on the dry side during winter, and should be watered only in spring and early summer when growing fast, and again at the end of summer to help the grass plump up good crowns for next year's bearing. Liquid manure from a farmyard is best ; in the absence of this an occasional light dressing of Peruvian guano is the next best, washing it in with a copious application of clean water.

Saving Seed of Onions

Q. I have some good Onions, grown from a prize strain, and wish to save seed. Kindly advise.—*Grower, Chertsey.*

A. Only bulbs of uniform shape and large size, according to the variety, should be selected for seed production. It is found in practice that new forms quickly deteriorate if selection is not rigidly carried out. February is the best time to plant the bulbs out, and a sheltered position in a rich soil should be chosen for them. So long as the soil is in a rich and fertile condition you need not add any more manure. Care should be taken to tie up the flower stalks, each to a stake, as soon as support is needed. The time to harvest depends upon the condition of the seed vessels ; thus, as soon as they begin to turn brown and to burst open, the heads should be cut off and dried in the sun. Afterwards place them in paper bags and suspend them from the roof of a cool and dry shed. The seed is readily cleaned, and may be kept for a season or two, but it cannot be depended upon afterwards.

Forcing Rhubarb

Q. Will you please tell me how to proceed to force Rhubarb ? —*M. K., Dartford.*

A. Rhubarb is one of the easiest of vegetables to force, and any structure having a temperature ranging from 55° to 60° may be used for the purpose ; or the roots may be covered in the open air with boxes 2 feet in height, having lids, and sufficiently wide to accommodate the crowns. Rhubarb pots, too, are often used. They may be bought at any pottery, and with care will last for years. The easiest method of forcing Rhubarb is to lift some strong roots and plant them in large pots or boxes, and place them under glass ; or the roots may be set moderately close together upon the ground, and covered with soil 2 inches above the crowns. Then give them a thorough soaking with water, to settle the soil among the roots. Afterwards, too, when in active growth, they must be well supplied with water, or the stems will be tough and stringy Any structure will suit Rhubarb, provided it has a warm, moist temperature. A forcing pit heated with hot water is, however, the best place for it where required in large quantities and of the very best quality. When forced in the open garden underneath pots or boxes, a heap of warm manure must be placed round each box. Where not forced, some long litter placed over the crowns early in spring will encourage early growth, when a few dishes may be had before the general crop comes into use.

Useful Winter Vegetables

Q. Could you give a list of useful winter vegetables with concise cultural directions ?—*Amery, Leeds.*

A. From a May sowing on a piece of good ground, and treated

like Carrots, splendid roots nearly 18 inches long of Salsafy or
Oyster Plant may be had by November. When properly cooked
and served they form a really excellent dish. Scorzonera requires
identical treatment, and where one is appreciated the other is sure
to be welcome. Good Turnips are often at a premium late in the
year, and Kohl Rabi makes a very good substitute. Sown in drills
in April, 15 inches apart and thinned out to 1 foot in the rows,
good roots will be available for winter use; the purple variety is
best for winter. They require more cooking than Turnips. While
every gardener is familiar with the ordinary Purple Sprouting variety
which proves so valuable in early spring, the merit of Christmas
Sprouting Broccoli for providing a dish at midwinter is sadly over-
looked. Plants from an early April sowing grow nearly 4 feet
across, and give an abundance of good sprouts to be cooked like
Asparagus during the festive season. It is more dwarf and compact
growing than the ordinary variety, and stands severe frosts with
impunity. Green Sprouting Broccoli is a great acquisition to the
winter vegetables. The young shoots are produced in great abundance, and if picked while young make a delicious vegetable, even
to those who often rate Winter Greens unpalatable. Stewed Celery
is well known, in fact, owing to the great demand for it, many
gardeners wish it were not so; it is a trifle disheartening to get
up nearly a dozen of one's best sticks, only to find later more
than half the stick has been thrown away. In such cases it will
be as well to try to introduce Celeriac, the roots of which make
a valuable winter vegetable, and do not require nearly so much
time spent upon them during the summer as Celery does.

Black Scab in Potatoes

Q. My Potatoes are attacked by the black scab disease. Can it
be cured ?—*E. O. H., Hants.*

A. The disease may be introduced with the seeds or sets, or it
may be present in the soil from a diseased crop. If scabbed
Potatoes are used for seed without having been sterilised, the result-
ing crop will almost certainly be diseased, and in addition the fungus
will pass into the soil, where it is capable of living for several years.
But scabbed Potatoes may be used for seed without the slightest
danger of spreading the disease if they are immersed for two hours
in a solution of ½ pint of commercial formalin (formaldehyde 40 per
cent.) mixed with 18 gallons of water. The Potatoes are then spread
out to dry, when they may be cut and planted in the usual manner·

Care must be taken after the Potatoes have been treated with the formalin solution that they are not used for food, and they should not be placed in sacks or hampers that have contained scabbed Potatoes. Land that has produced scabbed Potatoes should not be planted with Potatoes for several years afterwards. Beet, Swedes, Carrots, and Cabbages are also affected by the fungus ; cereals may be sown with safety on infected land. In the case of gardens and small allotments, where, of necessity, Potatoes are grown every year, the trenches in which the Potatoes are planted should be sprinkled with flowers of sulphur, this being done by means of a bellows apparatus. As you require 45 bushels of Potatoes for table use, you would need to plant $\frac{1}{4}$ acre, the produce of 1 acre of late Potatoes being about 6 tons, and 45 bushels equals $22\frac{1}{2}$ cwt., so that some margin will be left in excess to account for small or otherwise unusable tubers. It certainly pays allotment holders to grow their own Potatoes with land at 1s. per rod, £8 per acre, also many private and public establishments ; your cost of labour, however, is high, 24s. per week, and that may make just all the difference between economical and unremunerative production.

The Carrot Fly

Q. Please say what worm this is attacking my carrots. Some of the roots are a rusty brown colour, while others are rotten.—A. T. S., Colchester.

A. The worm is the larva or maggot of the Carrot fly. The fly does not, as a rule, attack them until the end of May. The flies appear in spring, and when the Carrot roots are well established the flies lay their eggs on them just below the ground. When full fed the maggots leave the roots for pupation in the soil ; the pupa case is light brown in colour, horny, and striated. There are several generations during the summer, but it is a remarkable fact that Carrots sown after the middle of July are seldom attacked, and good, useful Carrots are obtained by sowing about that time, say after early Potatoes. The freeing of the ground from pupae by dressing with gas lime in winter is an old fashioned preventive, but as the fly infests other umbelliferous plants the thing is to keep a sharp look out for the flies, and when they are seen about or on the Carrot plants, spray these with a solution of paraffin emulsion, 1 part of emulsion to 20 parts of water. This can be put on with a syringe having a spraying nozzle. To act preventively, spray the Carrot bed, after sowing, with the paraffin emulsion ; spray again with it after the plants are well above ground ; and a third time after thinning.

Mint During Winter

Q. How can I obtain a supply of Mint during winter ?—*Chester.*

A. Procure some boxes in which holes have been made for drainage, cover these with a large layer of leaves or short straw, then a layer of soil on top ; next lift some of the roots from the beds, shake off most of the old soil, then place them in boxes as close together as possible, covering them with 1 inch or so of soil. Any old potting soil will do. Give a good watering, after which place in a warm house. The roots will soon begin to produce an abundance of nice green shoots. In place of boxes, if so desired, pots may be substituted, and will often be found more convenient, especially where only a very small quantity is required. As there is often a demand for Mint before it comes on under natural conditions, this method of forcing is particularly handy, since it entails little or no trouble beyond a plentiful supply of moisture.

When and How to Form an Asparagus Bed

Q. Can you tell me the best time to plant Asparagus, and how to begin to form a bed ?—*S. A. G., Devon.*

A. The best time to plant Asparagus is during the month of April. Trench the ground in the autumn, and put in plenty of manure if the soil is poor in quality. Form low beds with shallow alleys between if the soil is light, and if it be heavy raise the beds 6 inches. Put out the plants in rows 15 inches apart, and 9 inches from plant to plant in the rows.

Tomato Fruits not Setting

Q. Can you tell me why the fruits fail to form on my Tomato plants in the greenhouse ? They bloom well, but instead of setting the flowers fall off.—*Anxious, Rye.*

A. The soil most probably needs a liberal dressing of lime. Do not plant Tomatoes in it again at least for a year. Instead of planting them in the border, plant them in boxes, tubs, or pots, using new soil, of course, and place them on the border. You will get quite as heavy crops ; at least, you will not be troubled with flowers falling. To prevent the further falling of your flowers we strongly advise you to give more air on warm days, leaving a little on also at night, and if possible have a little warmth in the hot water pipes at night.

The Tomato Disease

Q. Please enlighten me as to the cause of these large black patches on my Tomatoes, which are greatly disfigured?—*S. T. W., Richmond.*

A. Your Tomatoes have got the Tomato disease. It is the same thing as the Potato disease (Peronospora infestans). Pluck off and burn all the infested fruit; they are not fit for consumption. How the disease has come to attack your plants is difficult to tell, but we think the plants are too close together, or they have been allowed to become overcrowded with leafage, making it impossible for much air and light to permeate amongst the plants. Keeping the plants too wet at the root, and the atmosphere too damp, tends to bring on the disease. You should thin out the laterals and also some of the leaves to let in more light and air amongst the plants. Ventilate freely in warm weather, and on cold, wet days and nights you had better have a little heat in the hot water pipes, always with a little air on. If the disease has attacked the stems or leaves have the diseased parts dressed with flowers of sulphur.

Earthing Up Potatoes

Q. How and when should Potatoes be earthed up?—*Grateful, Exeter.*

A. To cover the young growing tops with a large bulk of soil, as obtains in some gardens, is decidedly a mistake, for in so doing many shoots get badly broken or knocked off, consequently the growth is checked, and the crop suffers. I like to earth up our Potatoes twice during the season. First, by gently drawing a little soil to them when a few inches above ground, and again three weeks later. Previous to the latter earthing we go over the whole plot and remove all superfluous growths from each root, leaving only the two strongest; at the same time a dressing of soot or wood ash is given. This during the earthing becomes incorporated with the soil, and has a wonderful influence on the foliage and the crop.

LIST OF ILLUSTRATIONS

INDEX

Printed in Great Britain
by Amazon